BLUE MOUNTAINS WORLD HERITAGE

BLUE MOUNTAINS
World Heritage

Text by Alex Colley

Photography by Henry Gold

COLONG FOUNDATION FOR WILDERNESS

Published by The Colong Foundation for Wilderness Ltd
2/362 Kent Street, Sydney NSW 2000
Telephone 02 9299 7341 Fax 02 9299 5713
Email: foundation@colongwilderness.org.au
Website: www.colongwilderness.org.au

© The Colong Foundation for Wilderness Ltd, 2004
Photographs © Henry Gold, 2004

All rights reserved. No part of this publication may be reproduced, stored in a retrieval system or transmitted in any form or by any means, electronic, mechanical, photocopying, recording or otherwise, except for brief extracts for the purpose of review, without the written permission of the publisher.

National Library of Australia Cataloguing-in-Publication
Colley, Alex, 1909- .
    Blue Mountains : World Heritage.
    Includes index.
    ISBN 0 85881 201 0.
    1. World Heritage areas – New South Wales – Blue Mountains.
    2. National parks and reserves – New South Wales – Blue Mountains. 3. Conservation of natural resources – New South Wales – Blue Mountains. I. Gold, Henry, 1934- .
    II. Colong Foundation for Wilderness. III. Title.
333.7816099445

Typesetting by Bungoona Technologies Pty Ltd, Grays Point NSW 2232.
Telephone 02 9526 6199.

Printed in China through Bookbuilders.

This book is set in 12/14.3 Bembo and is printed on Stora Enso chlorine-free paper products obtained from plantation forests.

The images in this book are available as archival prints. For orders contact the Colong Foundation for Wilderness.

FRONTISPIECE: Kanangra Gorge under low cloud.

A rocky overhang provides shelter for a variety of ferns.

Hard ironstone fluting has been revealed through weathering of the sandstone rock.

Foreword

THIS book celebrates one of the great achievements of the Australian conservation movement – the creation of the Greater Blue Mountains World Heritage Area.

For conservationists and governments it is an achievement that ranks with the protection of our rainforest reserves and the saving of the Franklin River as a landmark in the long and continuing struggle to preserve the unique places of the natural environment.

It was the late Milo Dunphy, with whom I enjoyed many walks in the Blue Mountains, who said that bushwalking, even for those who walked alone, could never be a solitary experience when we knew that countless others, now and in the future, could share the same pleasure and experience the same sights and sounds of the wild.

My Government is doing all it can to preserve those sights and sounds. Since coming to office, it has established to date 345 new national parks. Nearly six million hectares – over seven percent of the State's total land area – are covered in the national parks system.

For the Blue Mountains, World Heritage listing ensures that the beauty and grandeur of the region, its rivers and gorges and diverse species, are doubly safeguarded – by international covenant as well as Australian law. The Mountains now form part of a belt of conservation areas, from Brisbane Waters in the north to the Blue Mountains and the Royal National Park in the south, embracing Sydney in a great protective arc of verdant natural bushland. It is a priceless asset.

A landscape once known only to Aboriginal people, that later became the terrain of white explorers and later still the destination of countless tourists and holiday-makers, the Blue Mountains will now be preserved for the world. I congratulate the Colong Foundation for Wilderness on producing this handsome memento of the Blue Mountains World Heritage listing. I am proud of my Government's part in bringing the listing about and thank all who worked to achieve it.

BOB CARR
PREMIER OF NEW SOUTH WALES
MARCH 2004

Acknowledgements

MUCH of the information for this book came from individual contributions and from articles written by members of the Colong Foundation and contributed to the *Colong Bulletin*. Chapter 1, on the Dawn of Conservation, is derived from a paper by Jenny Ellis. Chapter 5, on the Wollemi, was written for the book by Haydn Washington. Chapter 6 on the Nattai and Gardens of Stone additions to the park system, Chapter 7 on the World Heritage campaign, and Chapter 9 on development threats were all heavily reliant on input from Keith Muir, Director of the Foundation. Keith led the campaigns for the World Heritage listing and the Nattai and Gardens of Stone National Parks. Jim Somerville's detailed critique of the first draft of the book made it much more readable. Pat Thompson's professional advice determined its format. The authors are indebted to Rod Richie for editing the book, and to Fiona McCrossin and Bob Walshe who proofread later drafts. The colour map of the Blue Mountains was provided by Australian Geographic's Cartographic Division and was expertly amended for the purposes of the publication by the Colong Foundation's honorary mapping draftsman, George Elliott.

The book has been made financially possible through a generous grant of $15,000 from the NSW Government to assist in promoting appreciation of the Greater Blue Mountains World Heritage Area. I would also like to thank Bob Debus, the Minister for the Environment and Member for the Blue Mountains, who organised the grant.

The book tells the story of how the Blue Mountains became World Heritage listed. The happy conclusion does not belong to any one group; it is a community achievement. It took 12 years to achieve World Heritage listing but, had it not been for conservation activities and campaigns dating back to the 19th century, the natural environment of the Blue Mountains would have been too degraded to qualify for this honour. While all care has been taken to obtain facts, check sources and meet the exacting requirements of contributors, any errors or omissions are the responsibility of the Colong Foundation.

ALEX COLLEY, OAM
Hon. Secretary
The Colong Foundation for Wilderness Ltd
Level 2, 362 Kent Street, Sydney 2000
web site: www.colongwilderness.org.au
email: foundation@colongwilderness.org.au

Contents

Introduction	1
Chapter 1 : The Dawn of Conservation	3
Chapter 2 : The Greater Blue Mountains	10
Chapter 3 : The Save Colong Campaign	18
Chapter 4 : The Boyd Campaign	36
Chapter 5 : Wollemi, and the Colo	52
Chapter 6 : Further Additions to the Park System	68
Chapter 7 : The World Heritage Campaign	84
Chapter 8 : Threats to the World Heritage Area	102
Chapter 9 : Celebration and Dedication	112
Index	124

The black and white images accompanying the text were used in the campaigns described.

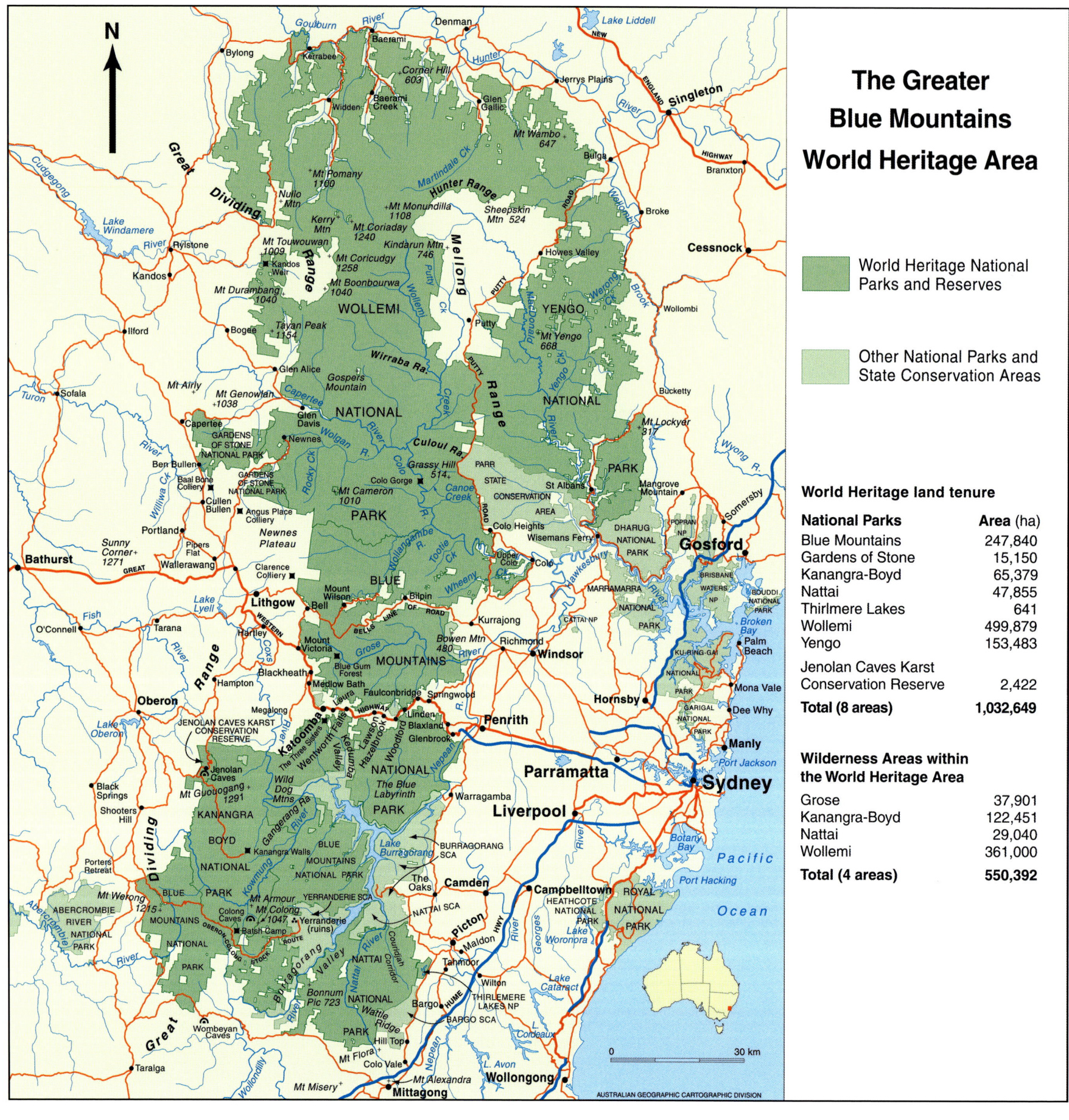

Introduction

A WORLD Heritage nomination for the Greater Blue Mountains, in Australia's most populous state New South Wales, was completed and presented to UNESCO in June 1998. It was lodged nearly nine years after a detailed report prepared by Dr Geoff Mosley and followed a long series of reviews, assessments and assessments of assessments, interspersed by delays occasioned by government inertia. International World Heritage expert, the late H.C. (Bing) Lucas, described the nomination as one of the best ever presented. Though more detailed than Geoff Mosley's submission, it was however less comprehensive. It played down the geomorphological significance of the Blue Mountains, instead emphasising their value as 'an outstanding example of temperate eucalypt dominated forest and woodland'. The nomination, extending over one million hectares of parkland, was unanimously accepted by UNESCO's twenty-one-nation World Heritage Committee at its twenty-fourth session in Cairns on 29 November 2000.

Perhaps the most significant factor in winning the support of the Committee was the lobby book illustrated with Henry Gold photographs which, in view of the eucalypt-dominated theme of the nomination, quoted the support of 12 eminent botanists and ecologists.

The nomination describes the Greater Blue Mountains as representing 'an extraordinary story of natural antiquity, diversity, beauty and human attachment…an environment in which key aspects of Australia's exceptional natural and cultural histories are protected and presented to a wide spectrum of the public… The integrity of the area is fully protected. Its legal status is that of eight publicly owned protected areas, which include large areas of protected wilderness.' The nomination explains the area's conformity to the five World Heritage criteria, any one of which may establish the outstanding universal value of a natural heritage property.

The first criterion is that an area must be an *outstanding example representing major stages of earth's history, including the record of life, significant ongoing geological processes in the development of land form, or significant geomorphic or physiographic features.* The dissected Greater Blue Mountains sandstone plateaus are described as an intriguing example of all these aspects of the earth's evolution. These were its geological beginnings through convergent (active) margin tectonics, its uplift through the subsequent divergent (passive) margin, its dissection through the cutting of the gorges, and its extraordinarily diverse features, from pagoda-like formations to limestone caves. The nomination, however, did not seek World Heritage listing for the sandstone landforms because Australia's scientific opinion had, at that time, been divided on key aspects of the area's geology.

The second criterion is that an area must be an *outstanding example representing significant ongoing ecological and biological processes in the evolution and development of terrestrial, fresh water, coastal and marine ecosystems and communities of plants and animals.* The Mountains are described as 'the centre of diversity of eucalypts' and 'a globally outstanding example of species divergence occurring in a relatively small area'. Its local endemism is among the highest in the world for a temperate forest region, with 114 plant species endemic to the nominated area.

The third criterion is that an area must *contain natural phenomena or areas of exceptional natural beauty and aesthetic importance.* The natural phenomena of the Mountains are described as 'superlative' and this natural beauty has inspired not only creative artists but everyone else.

The fourth criterion is that an area must *contain the most important and significant natural habitats for in-situ conservation of biological diversity, including threatened species of outstanding universal value from the view of science or conservation.* The Mountains are 'the most biologically diverse part of the Eastern Sclerophyll Open Forest', containing the world's most outstanding representation of eucalypt-dominated communities. More than 120 vascular plant species or subspecies are considered to be rare or threatened, including the Wollemi pine (*Wollemia nobilis*).

The fifth criterion addresses cultural associations. An area must be *directly or tangibly associated with events or living conditions, with ideas or with beliefs, with artistic and literary works of outstanding universal significance.* The nomination of cultural associations linked the area's natural attributes to its Aboriginal background and conservation history. The area is described as having 'universal value for the scientific significance of its suite of some 700 known Aboriginal occupational and rock art sites across extensive undisturbed areas'. Four phases of voluntary conservation efforts are described as:
- The health-based movement in the 1870s which resulted in the first parks and the track systems;
- The bushwalker conservation movement of the 1930s, out of which came the large visionary parks and wilderness reserve proposals;
- The conservation revival of the 1960s which created mass public support for the implementation of the earlier large park proposals and the wilderness reserves; and
- The 1990s move to consolidate and confirm environmental values including the recognition of World Heritage values.

The book is mostly about those voluntary conservation efforts. It has been written from the standpoint of the Colong Foundation for Wilderness, because the Foundation was responsible for the World Heritage listing proposal and led the subsequent campaign which was strongly supported by many other organisations (see Environment Minister Bob Debus' speech reported in Chapter 9). The Colong Foundation decided in the 1980s to seek World Heritage listing. It then approached Dr Geoff Mosley to frame a proposal. The Foundation itself financed Dr Mosley's book, *Blue Mountains for World Heritage,* which was launched by the Hon. Bob Carr in 1989. It took another 11 years of persistent campaigning to achieve listing. Half a century ago the Cumberland County Council planned a 'green belt' on Sydney's urban fringe. It soon lost out to development, but the city now has a green belt, consisting mostly of national parks. The largest and most scenic component is the Blue Mountains. This feature is significant, not only for the protection of much of Sydney's water catchment and its eucalypt diversity, but for the State's economy through tourism.

A view from the Red Rocks toward the heart of the Wollemi Wilderness.

CHAPTER 1

The Dawn of Conservation

researched by Jenny Ellis

WORLD Heritage listing for the Blue Mountains was only made possible by the sustained efforts of many thousands of people over the last two centuries. We owe a great deal to the early conservationists who fought for protective legislation and campaigned for the first reserves.

For the early immigrants to NSW, mainly from the British Isles, the ideal landscape was a fertile green sward with some coppices and occasional patches of remnant forest. Cliff-lined plateaus, incised with deep gorges and covered in 'untidy' eucalypts, were regarded as wastelands. While earlier colonial governments valued them as outer 'prison walls' that helped contain escaped convicts, the areas were mostly seen as a barrier to development.

Governor King, in a dispatch written in 1805, said that the Mountains were 'a confused and barren assemblage'. The extension of agriculture would have to be curtailed because the rocks of the range 'were the most barren and forbidding aspect which men, animals, birds and vegetation has ever been stranger to'. In *Natural Sketches of New South Wales,* published in 1844, Mrs Charles Meredith wrote:

> We continued our journey through a wild and barren country, utterly destitute of herbage, the inhospitable Blue Mountains were before, behind, and on either side of us, rising in grand and dreary monotony of form and colour. Forests of tall gums covered them from base to peak, but instead of beauty in the landscape, there was deformity. All bore the marks of fire far up their branchless blackened stems, and in many places the burning had been so recent that for miles the very earth seemed charred and not even a stunted shrub had sprung up again.

However, many notable observers were deeply impressed by the scenery and geomorphology of the Mountains. They included Gregory Blaxland, Paul Strezlecki, Thomas Mitchell, Charles Darwin and the geologist Dwight Dana. In the journal describing his 1836 visit, Darwin described the Mountains as striking, magnificent and profound. He wrote:

> A sound of pouring water reached us, the cause of which was soon explained by one of the most stupendous scenes I ever beheld, bursting unexpectedly upon us. Suddenly we found ourselves standing on the brink of a tremendous precipice... It is not easy to conceive a more magnificent spectacle than that presented to a person walking on the summit plain, when, without any notice, he arrives at the brink of one of these cliffs which are so perpendicular that he can strike with a stone (as I have tried) the trees growing at a depth of between one thousand and one thousand five hundred feet below him.

And in 1850 Dana wrote in an article in the *American Journal of Science and Arts:*

> The great depth, extent and number of the valleys of New South Wales are calculated to excite wonder, and perplex us much in the study of their origin. In some of the sandstone regions the gorges intersect the country in endless succession, with usually inaccessible precipices of one, two or three thousand feet. They are deep gulfs with walled sides composed of horizontal layers of sandstone. The layers seem to have been continuous and what is the force which has channelled the mountain structure? Are they stupendous rents in the bosom of the earth? Are they regions of subsidence? Can it be that they were never filled but were depressions left between the heaps of accumulating sediment that constitute the sandstone, which

depressions were often enlarged by sea during the elevation of the land? Or may we adopt the 'preposterous' idea that simply running water has been the agent, and if so was it fresh water, or the ocean?

In the 19th century, as now, there were many who put damaging recreational activities before conservation. In his book, *Ten Years With Palette, Shotgun and Rifle on the Mountains,* published in 1899, S.R. Bellingham wrote that occasionally while he was hunting, the beauty of the landscape would arouse his artistic sensibility. 'These hunting fits were recurrent during my whole shooting career…such was the beauty of the scenery that I would be tempted to copy it and return once more to the hunting life.' Even though he acknowledged that every year the native game of Australia was getting less, he continued to shoot and advise his readers on the best way to shoot a platypus. Such paradoxes were common. A prevalent attitude of the time was that a reserve had to be cleared to make it valuable. During the 19th century much damage was inflicted on the natural environment of the Mountains. D.H. Keith and D.H. Benson, in an article published in *Cunninghamia* in 1988, wrote:

The continuous high cliffs of the central Blue Mountains, as seen in the Grose Valley, have inspired both artists and scientists since the middle of the 19th century.

Kanangra Deep, Kanangra-Boyd National Park.

The Blue Mountains has seen decades of unsustainable logging and indiscriminate clearing of trees. In valleys and on level terrain, native flora has been removed entirely and replaced. Where forests remain, the forest giants have been removed. There was already a noticeable decline in native shrubs in the 1890s. Several long-time residents of the Blue Mountains, including Billy Lynch, reported that once plentiful 'native fruits' had all but vanished in the last 30 years (*Sydney Mail* 1896). By the late 20th century, at least 68 native plants were listed as rare, threatened or locally vulnerable to extinction in the region.

Protection of the native flora and fauna was attempted by two measures. The first was the prohibition of hunting. The *Animal Protection Act* of 1879 outlawed the hunting of a number of game birds during the breeding season. In 1881, this Act was replaced by the *Birds Protection Act* which was amended in 1901 to outlaw the hunting of some native birds for a five-year period, and protect other species during the breeding season. The *Native Animals Protection Act, 1903* saw the first legal protection given to native animals in NSW. There were 'closed seasons' for the hunting of wallaroos, koalas, wombats, echidnas, platypus, grey kangaroos and gliding possums. The *Birds Protection Act, 1901* had, by 1905, listed 100 species of native birds that were absolutely protected for a period of ten years. In 1918 a combined *Birds and Animals Protection Act* protected all native animals not considered noxious.

The Three Sisters, Katoomba's popular tourist attraction, has become the worldwide symbol for the Blue Mountains.

Where the sun's rays strike the Grose Valley lies the Blue Gum Forest, cradle of the modern conservation movement in Australia.

In such a large area as the Mountains, police enforcement of these protection Acts was impractical. In the *Blue Mountains Echo* of 8 November 1921, Ruth Schliecher wrote:

> The *Birds and Animals Act, 1918* is hopelessly ineffective owing to the lack of public sentiment in their favour, for public opinion is the life and strength of the law, and especially such laws as these, which cannot be publicly administered by the police without the people and in such a sparsely populated country as Australia.

Public appreciation of the Mountains was largely determined by their accessibility. In the days of horse-drawn transport it took a day to reach Penrith from Sydney and a day or more to traverse the Mountains. The construction of the railway line to Penrith in 1863 brought the Mountains a day nearer to Sydney, and the completion of the line to Mount Victoria in 1867 brought the Mountains within a few hours of the city. The NSW Government Railways promoted tourism. The *Railway Guide,* published in 1879, described the Mountains:

> The Blue Mountains, with their innumerable hills and ravines, present extensive panoramas of the greatest description. As the traveller in the railway is sped along the summit of the range and catches glimpses of the thousand valleys, stretching out like ocean waves to the horizon, on both sides of the line which, for a considerable distance, is laid on a narrow causeway that looks as if built for thousands of feet out of awful depths of precipice and ravine, he finds it difficult to imagine a nobler representation of the grandeur and sublimity of nature.

With the completion of the railway, one of the earliest constructed in Australia, the Mountains soon became the State's most favoured tourist destination, and although their popularity declined during the 20th century, many of the hotels and boarding houses constructed in the early days are still operative and some two million people visit the Mountains every year. An essential tourist facility was a network of walking tracks, which enabled visitors to reach favoured lookout points easily. The first tracks were initiated by Sir Henry Parkes and other notables attracted to the Mountains. Walking became popular and the participants often promoted conservation efforts.

A number of reserves were established, although they were small in comparison with the national parks created in the second half of the 20th century. The first was Jenolan Caves, gazetted in 1866. In 1867 a reserve of 11,380 hectares, stretching from Lawson to Mount Victoria, was created, although it was later reduced to only 1,712 hectares. Perhaps the most significant reservation was that of the Grose Valley for water supply purposes, though this did not rule out agricultural and mining development. By 1914 there were 79 recreation grounds and reserves covering 7,859 hectares. Details of the walking tracks constructed, and the reservations dedicated, are available in the book *Fauna of the Blue Mountains* by J. and P. Smith and in Dr T.J. Daly's unpublished thesis, *Elements of the Past: An Environmental History of the Blue Mountains, Australia*.

The enjoyment of the Mountains by walkers, tourists, writers, artists, scientists, and many others, laid the foundation for the increasing appreciation that culminated in World Heritage listing.

Warm temperate rainforest flourishes in the shady recesses found along the many escarpments in the Blue Mountains.

CHAPTER 2

The Greater Blue Mountains

THE Blue Mountains extend for over 200 km across the dissected terrain of sandstone plateaus west of Sydney, from the Hunter Valley south to Mount Alexandra, adjoining Mittagong. During the 19th century, tourism was confined mostly to the vicinity of the Mountain towns. Only stockmen and cattle duffers visited small areas of the thousands of square kilometres beyond the towns.

Whilst reservations were few, they included the Grose Valley, Jenolan Caves and small scattered areas in the vicinity of the towns. These reservations saved important natural areas from development and enabled the public to gain an appreciation for the environment. The vast areas north and south of the central townships were generally not appreciated until they became favoured territory for bushwalkers.

The first walking club to use the Blue Mountains, the Warragamba Club, founded in 1895, walked mainly on roads and tracks and used overnight lodgings. The first club to engage in walks taking days or even weeks was the Mountain Trails Club, formed by Myles Dunphy, Roy Rudder and Bert Gallop in 1914. It was inevitable that the pioneer walkers of the clubs would be concerned that their favourite areas were threatened with development. In 1932 they formed the National Parks and Primitive Areas Council, which included representatives from four bushwalking clubs. Its objectives included: locating and planning areas suitable for national parks; categorisation of national parks into primitive areas and areas for motor tourists; and opposition to commercial interests within the areas proposed for protection.

In 1934, in a supplement to the *Katoomba Daily*, Myles Dunphy published his plan for a Greater Blue Mountains National Park. In the foreword he wrote:

> The Blue Mountains of Australia are justly famous for their grand scenery of stupendous canyons and gorges, mountain peaks and plateaux up to 4,000 feet altitude, uncounted thousands of ferny, forested dells and gauzy waterfalls, diversified forest and river beauty, much aloof wilderness – and towns and tourist resorts replete with every convenience for the comfort and entertainment of both Australian and overseas visitors.

He summarised the proposal as follows:
> The Blue Mountains National Park proposal is that all the unalienated – inferior – Crown lands of the Greater Blue Mountains region, from Mts Boonbourwa, Durambang and Uraterer (Gospers Mountain) in the north to Mt Werong, Wombat Pinch, Bonnum Pic, Colong, Yerranderie Peak, Mt Cumbertine and Couridjah in the south, be set apart and dedicated as the Blue Mountains National Park, for the purposes of preservation of scenery and areas of natural bushland, for conservation of wildlife, and for the furtherance of all kinds of recreation not destructive of the essentials of the proposal.

His proposal was inspired by conservation developments in the United States where, he wrote, 'the wonderful and natural adjuncts of that great nation were being ruthlessly destroyed in the middle of the 19th century'. In 1872, the Yellowstone was created as the first large public park, with an area of 887,300 hectares. In 1890, Yosemite (300,946 ha), Sequoia (156,430 ha) and General Grant (1,036 ha) were reserved. Subsequently, 22 parks with a total area of 3,290,468 hectares were dedicated. In Africa, the Kruger National Park in the Transvaal had an area of 2,204,005 hectares. Dunphy's proposal was on a scale not previously envisaged in Australia, although other large parks, such as Kosciuszko, the Border

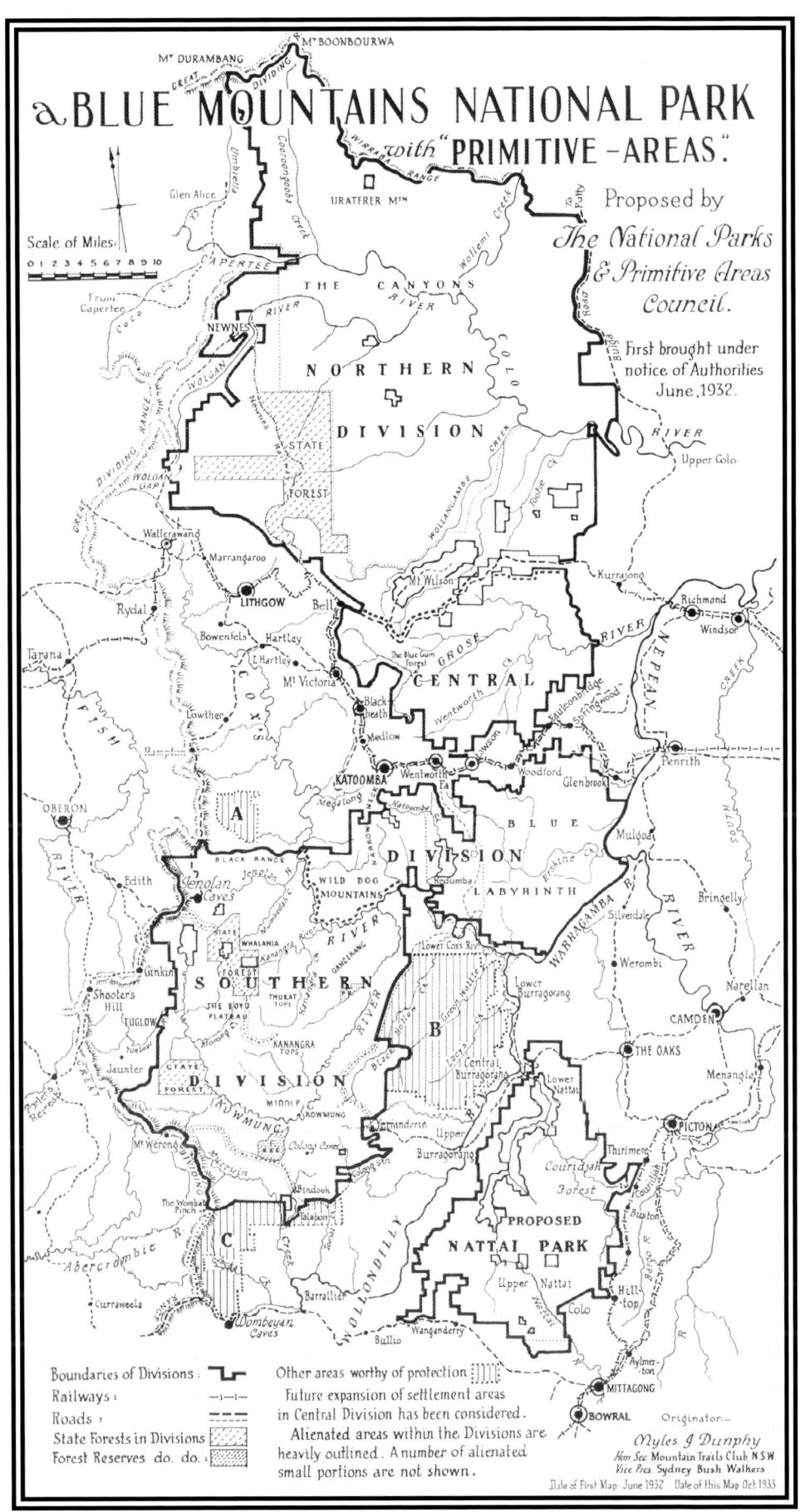

Ranges and Morton-Budawang were later established. Previously, reservations such as the Royal National Park and Ku-ring-gai Chase had been dedicated, and these had an invaluable role in preserving areas near the fringe of Sydney which otherwise would have been sacrificed to urban expansion. These reservations also increased public appreciation of nature conservation. The Greater Blue Mountains National Park proposal was, however, on a different plane.

Dunphy saw the mountains as 'potential desert land' which, 'if not for specialised hardy vegetation, would be a vast rocky region of bad lands'. He wrote that 'more surface rock was exposed than ever before in memory and indigenous fauna was much depleted. The premier scenic area of Australia and playground of Australia is fast being subjugated, in fact being subjugated by various private interests, lawful and unlawful'.

Dunphy's claim that 'This is the age of conservation' was premature. The battle against development of natural areas in the Blue Mountains and elsewhere has proven to be unending. However, he did cover the concerns of today's conservationists with a constantly recurring theme in his proposal – the preservation of wilderness. National parks would be designated as roadless primitive areas and 'tourist open areas in which motor tourists would be accommodated'. He proposed a primitive area in the Southern Division of the Park, most of which was later included in the Kanangra-Boyd Wilderness, and others in the Blue Labyrinth, the Nattai and the Grose Valley. He did not propose a wilderness in the Northern Division, which he described as 'very little known'. He proposed that many areas in the vicinity of towns and roads be designated tourist open areas. In a remarkably prescient statement in the days before four wheel drive vehicles and commercial horseriding tours, he opposed 'recreation damaging to the essentials of the proposal'.

While the Greater Blue Mountains National Park proposal was in preparation, another seminal conservation event took place. In April 1931, a party of Mountain Trails Club and Sydney Bush Walkers members reached the junction of the Grose River and Govetts Leap Creek, the site of a magnificent Blue Gum Forest situated, in Dunphy's words, 'in the very centre of what is now regarded as the major tourist scenic feature in Australia'. They were horrified to find that ringbarking of the forest had already started. This triggered a campaign which, together with the Garawarra campaign, marked in his words 'the rise of a new conservation dawn in the land'. A combined committee, led by Dunphy and Alan Rigby, was formed and negotiated, with C.A. Hungerford, the purchase of his conditional purchase lease that covered the forest. Mr Hungerford had intended to grow walnuts on the land, but agreed to sell the lease for 150 pounds, which seemed a high price for unimproved land remote from roads. He settled for a price of 130 pounds, but stipulated that it should be paid within six weeks. For two small clubs to raise a sum equal to over $10,000 dollars today, within 6 weeks, in the middle of the Great Depression, was a daunting task. However, they approached Mr W.J. Cleary, Commissioner for Railways, an enthusiastic bushwalker and conservationist, for a loan. He lent 80 pounds – which apparently he didn't expect to get back, although the loan was repaid a year later. And so, in Dunphy's words, 'ended a successful epic struggle to secure for the outdoor public a piece of natural paradise which any staff surveyor in the first place and at a glance should have recognised as being a priceless gem of bushland beauty in a unique scenic situation'. The land was given back to the Crown. The Blue Gum Forest Reserve 60521 for Public Recreation was notified on 2 November 1932, and regulations for its management appeared in the *Government Gazette* in March 1934. Blue Gum Forest was the first instalment of the Greater Blue Mountains National Park.

A potent means of promoting the Greater Blue Mountains National Park proposal was the large scale detailed maps, masterpieces of artistic drafting, which Dunphy published. One of these was of the Bindook Highland, Colong Maze, Tomat Heights, Bindook Gorge, the Talabon and the Southern Kowmung. Another was of Gangerang, Wild Dog Mountains, Lower Kowmung and North Thurat. Both maps were on a scale of two inches to the mile. Although it was impossible to provide contours, cliff

Asgard Swamp in the Blue Mountains National Park. Many endemic, rare and endangered plants are restricted to the upland swamps of the central Blue Mountains.

lines were depicted and the steepness of slopes was well shown by finely detailed hachuring. Heights of the higher features and some of the prominent lower features were given, and it was known that the rivers, except in their higher reaches, were only a few hundred feet above sea level. Of much greater scope and circulation was the Blue Mountains and Burragorang map, on a scale of half an inch to the mile, published by the Department of Lands. The map covered the Southern Blue Mountains as far south as Berrima and west to Oberon and Taralga. Much, if not most, of the data was supplied by Dunphy, who for a year spent several days a week working with the Department draftsman, Mr Arthur Cooke. At first the Department was against a map on so large a scale. Its maps were to serve 'the public', which in the Thirties meant the motoring public. Dunphy wanted a map which would serve the needs of the fast growing bushwalking movement. He wrote that, 'One of my guiding reasons (for the map) was that if the outdoors public, including motorists and motor campers, were ever to get a great national park in the Greater Blue Mountains region, the promoters would need a map which would show the main scenic and other features identifiable for identification and discussion'. The map was in exactly the same style as Dunphy's own maps, with depiction of negotiable routes and trails. The maps boosted visitor numbers, particularly of bushwalkers. Despite the subsequent publication of half inch to the mile military maps and 1 in 25,000 maps, they feature attributes not named on the later maps and are still used by bushwalkers.

The efforts of bushwalking conservationists in the early 1930s saved the magnificent Blue Gum Forest in the heart of the Grose Wilderness. The campaign proved to be the starting point for future successful community campaigns that preserved the Greater Blue Mountains Area.

View of Mount Caley across the heath-covered slopes of Mount Hay. Such mesa-tops and heathlands are the key locality for the Mountains' many rare plants.

It is not surprising that Dunphy's plan, which was far ahead of its time, attracted little support for many years, except from bushwalkers and the Katoomba Council. But it was a meticulously researched and detailed plan which provided reliable guidance for the infant nature conservation movement. Over the next 30 years, there were both favourable and unfavourable developments.

In October 1937, the Minister for Lands gazetted Reserve 67062 of 23,288 hectares, about half of the Boyd Plateau. It was gazetted as a reserve for the preservation of flora and fauna, but although the Forestry Department had entered into an agreement not to allow logging without the consent of the Lands Department, it was heavily logged for 8 years. The construction of the road to Kanangra Walls was completed in 1940, a dagger of development penetrating to the heart of the later declared Kanangra-Boyd Wilderness. The Narrow Neck Peninsula was threatened with roading and possible residential development. This was strongly opposed by the bushwalking movement. The Peninsula was used by bushwalkers in the days when they didn't own cars, as a pathway to the Kanangra-Boyd Wilderness. They travelled by train to Katoomba on Friday nights and camped at Diamond Falls, Corral Swamp or Clear Hill. The threat did not eventuate, Narrow Neck being added to the park in 1987. Favourable developments included the establishment of the National Parks Association in 1957 and the creation of the National Parks and Wildlife Service in 1967. However, it was not until 1959 that the first section of the Greater Blue Mountains National Park was declared. The Blue Mountains National Park protected the popular tourism areas near the towns and included most of the Central Division of Dunphy's plan. The Colong Caves and Boyd campaigns of the late Sixties and early Seventies, directed against destructive development proposals, were the turning point for the Greater Blue Mountains National Park proposal.

The Blue Breaks from Mount Colong. The vast Blue Mountains wilderness landscapes are spellbinding.

Blue Mountains Ash (Eucalyptus oreades) *is found on sheltered slopes and gullies above 800 metres.*

CHAPTER 3
The Save Colong Campaign

COLONG Caves are situated in the Kowmung River Valley. However, the 40,000 hectare Kanangra-Boyd National Park, which was created in 1969 and covered a large part of the Southern Division of Dunphy's Greater Blue Mountains National Park proposal, importantly omitted the Colong Caves and most of the Boyd Plateau. A few years before, the Metropolitan Cement Company had developed a plan to mine the limestone around the caves, thereby creating a situation similar to that of clearing the Blue Gum Forest, though on a much greater scale. Both proposals would have scarred otherwise pristine valleys. The limestone mine would have been a blot on the landscape when viewed from many points in the surrounding parklands.

The appeal of the area, both to bushwalkers and the cement company, was its accessibility. It is only 40 km in a direct line from the Cumberland Plain. The central city buildings, the Harbour Bridge and the lights of the metropolis are clearly visible from certain high points within the wilderness. The special value of the site to the cement company was its proximity to the Maldon cement works, 50 km away. Due to the rugged intervening terrain, the conveyance of the limestone to the works may have cost more than transport from some of the 300 deposits elsewhere in the State, especially those adjacent to railways. Between the Caves and Maldon are the Burragorang Valley, about 500 metres deep, and the Nattai Valley and the Couridjah Corridor, each of about the same depth. The cost of a railway would have been prohibitive, so the preferred mode of transport was a slurry pipeline. No cost estimates were ever produced; nor was the feasibility of lifting the slurry from the valleys addressed, nor the environmental effects, including erosion, of pipeline construction.

Colong Caves were reserved from sale in 1899 and declared as Reserve 29837 for the preservation of caves in 1928. The reserve was also proclaimed a 'bird and animal' sanctuary. In 1939, the Department of Mines was considering the granting of mineral leases within the reserve for the extraction of limestone. Following protests by the National Parks and Primitive Areas Council, the area was re-dedicated in November 1939 as R68800 for public recreation and preservation of caves. An assurance from the Under Secretary for Mines that the mineral leases had been refused, 'being considered inimical to public interest', was believed to have placed the caves beyond the reach of mining interests. In 1956, however, it was learned that a number of mining applications within the County of Westmoreland (which included Colong) were under consideration. The Mountain Trails Club lodged strong protests, but three leases were granted within the reserve. These were considered by the lessee, Portland Cement, to be too small and inaccessible for economic exploitation, and the conservation societies hoped they would not be developed.

In May 1965 a party of Sydney Bush Walkers came upon a large permanent camp near the head of Colong Swamp. The camp was unoccupied, but there were many specimens of limestone in well-made boxes. The Federation of Bushwalking Clubs took up the matter with the Department of Mines and registered a formal objection to drilling or mining in R68800. The camp may have been set up by Theiss Bros, who had applied for a permit to prospect for limestone. Loder and Dunphy, Sydney architects, also lodged strong objections.

Myles Dunphy again entered the fray. He did not object to quarrying in 'indifferent surroundings' where the enterprise 'had no connotation with scenic beauty and produced useful products', but incidentals of large-scale quarrying were intolerable in the Kanangra-Boyd Wilderness. He described the incidentals as:

View from Kanangra Tops looking south over the Kowmung Valley to Mount Colong on the horizon.

The bedlam of explosive blasts, of drills and crushers, of creaking and groaning machinery, of hooters and shrieks, of time whistles that penetrate far into the peaceful ranges. Also there are the sights that assault the eye, the smashed face of nature, the works, sheds, machinery, roads, tracks, services, cables, posts and wires, drains and fences, in mostly graded hillsides, huts clustered in hollows and terraces, and sludge, dead trees and rubbish choking the beds of narrow gullies.

In January 1967 a further mining lease (ML46) covering Church Creek and Mount Armour at the northern end of the caves reserve, together with a permit to prospect over an area adjacent to the existing leases, was granted to Portland Cement by the Minister for Lands, the Hon. Tom Lewis. The Minister was also the Member for Wollondilly, in which the Colong Caves Reserve was situated. The lease terms included a rental of $23 a year and royalty of 5 cents a tonne.

The Askin Government's intention, which was evident in October 1966, aroused strong opposition. The Federation of Bushwalking Clubs, the National Trust, the National Parks Association, the Institute of Architects and others sent letters to the press and politicians. By 1968 the campaign had attracted editorials from the *Sydney Morning Herald (SMH)* and the *Daily Telegraph* which were strongly supportive. An *SMH* editorial of 4 May stated that 'Mr Fife (Minister for Mines) has been at pains to tell us that the company's lease lies outside the boundaries of the Kanangra-Boyd National Park. It lies outside them because the Government has lopped 5,000 acres [2,000 ha] from the park in order to make way for it'. The editorial concluded:

> Already we can see in the dwindling fertility of the soil, the increasing destructiveness of floods, droughts, deforestation and the extinction of exploited species, the stripping of plant and forest cover from the land, the pollution of air, lakes and rivers by industrial and human waste, the consequences of centuries of uncontrolled exploitation. If the Government can be brought to see that the issue of Colong runs deeper than the price of cement, the dispute may not have been in vain.

In 1967 the National Parks Association issued a brochure titled 'Quarry Valuable Scenery?'; the Sydney University Conservation Society organised a petition to Parliament with over 8,000 signatures; the Nature Conservation Council of NSW attempted to bring the dispute before a Mining Warden's Court; and a number of architects advised their clients against using the cement of Associated Portland Cement, the parent company of Metropolitan Portland Cement.

In May 1968 Milo Dunphy (son of Myles) organised a meeting of over 50 conservation societies, chaired by Professor R.N. Johnson, held in Sydney University Union Hall. The following resolutions were passed unanimously:
- We deplore the decision of the New South Wales Government to excise part of the Colong Caves Reserve and environs (totalling 5,000 acres) from the proposed Kanangra-Boyd National Park;
- We believe that quarrying and associated works in the Colong Reserve will despoil the wilderness character of the greater part of the proposed Kanangra-Boyd Park;
- We reject the assertion of the Government that this decision is in the interest of the nation and condemn the short sightedness of the Government in sacrificing the most important scenic wilderness remaining in New South Wales;
- We call on the Government and Parliament to review Cabinet's decision to allow mining in Colong Caves Reserve and include the Reserve in Kanangra-Boyd National Park and thus demonstrate the sincerity of its concern for the preservation of the natural heritage of the State and the recreational needs of the expanding community; and
- We ask for a public inquiry to enable consideration of all aspects of the matter.

Upper Kalang Falls in the Kanangra-Boyd Wilderness.

It was also resolved that a 'Colong Committee' be appointed. A little over a year later the Committee adopted a second objective: to stop the establishment of a pine forest on the Boyd Plateau. The Committee elected Father James Tierney from the Catholic Bushwalkers as its Chairman, N.F.A. Keen OBE as Secretary, and Milo Dunphy as Press Secretary. The Committee was faced with a daunting task, but, as it stated in *Colong Bulletin* No. 15: 'If we cannot preserve the most highly dedicated public reserve in the State, at the most focal point of our best national park, together with the hub and catchment of that park, we cannot preserve anything'. The Committee had to start from scratch. It had no experience in conducting what was essentially a major conservation campaign, because there had never been one before. It soon comprehended the essential features of campaigning and invented many original methods of achieving its aim. A barrage of disparagement of its members was evoked. They were described as 'ratbags', 'eco-nuts', 'eco-freaks', 'radical extremists' and 'elitists', despite the fact that a large proportion of the Committee and its supporters were well qualified professionals. The ultimate expression of contempt was to describe them as 'emotional'. Several of them were later to be awarded Order of Australia honours.

Essential for a successful campaign is to establish the facts beyond question. The National Parks Association had already researched the reservation history of the Caves. Within two months of its appointment, the Committee had commissioned a firm of consultant geologists to report on geological aspects of the controversy and had received the first stage of its report. The Sydney Speleological Society, a strong supporter of the Committee, located three cave systems in the Church Creek area of

Today's unspoilt view from Kanangra Tops across the Kowmung Valley to Mt Colong. If limestone mining had proceeded, there would have been an open cut mine on Mt Armour in the centre of this picture, with a road and power line leading to the mine, and a sludge pipeline over the ridges to the cement works beyond the horizon.

The pure waters of the Kowmung River reveal every rock and shingle beneath its surface.

the Colong Caves Reserve. It also discovered an underground river and an endangered species of rock wallaby. Although the existence of caves in the Church Creek area had been reported to the Department of Mines by Mr O. Trickett in 1899, the Hon. Wal Fife, Minister for Mines, denied that the caves would be affected. The largest cave, 430 metres long, was then named the 'Fife Cave' by its discoverers. Ten other caves were named after government ministers.

The Committee's geological survey estimated that nearby limestone deposits, about the same distance from Maldon as Colong, contained 50 million tonnes of limestone, whereas the Mines Department estimated the deposit as being only 600,000 tonnes. This was vital information because, by October 1969, Minister Fife had announced that the Colong leases would be cancelled if other sites proved satisfactory. Within two years the Department admitted that the Committee's estimate was conservative, with 60–70 million tonnes being nearer the mark.

A report was also commissioned from L.N. Jamieson, in association with Laurie and Montgomery, Consulting Engineers. The report revealed that, although 150 km of road was required for the project (for access, the slurry pipeline, power lines and other uses), and this would create a 'major erosion hazard', the Soil Conservation Service had not been consulted, nor had the opinion of the National Parks and Wildlife Service been sought. The slurry pipeline would also create erosion hazards in steeply sloping country.

The campaign was fought on three fronts – against the Government, against the cement company, and for the support of the media.

Although several discussions were held with Minister Fife, and with the Minister for Conservation, Mr Beale, the question was not resolved by these means. The Premier, Mr Askin, refused to meet a deputation. Ministers of the succeeding Labor Government, and its Premier, were accessible to Committee deputations and on occasion sought the advice of Committee members.

The Kowmung River, in the very heart of the southern Blue Mountains, was to be dammed to provide water for a pipeline to pump a slurry of crushed limestone to the cement works.

Seen from Crafts Wall, Mt Cloudmaker lives up to its name.

At the Georges River by-election, held in November 1970, 10,000 copies of a leaflet attacking the Government's policy were distributed. In response to queries from the Committee, the Liberal candidate, Mr Tonkin, expressed the hope that alternative sites for limestone deposits would prove a practical alternative to Mount Armour.

The policy of the Committee at the State election held early in 1971 was to make voters aware of the Colong-Boyd issue by the distribution of pamphlets, by articles and letters to the local press, and by petitions and meetings. Supporters were asked to obtain clear statements from all candidates on the action they would take on the issue if elected. Three members of the Committee stood as Australia Party candidates – Milo Dunphy in Miranda, David Eden in Ashfield and Brian Walker in Premier Askin's electorate of Collaroy. The Australia Party's policy was to revoke both the mining leases in the reserve and the Konangaroo forest on the Boyd (the site of the proposed pine plantation) and add both areas to the Kanangra Boyd National Park. The main value of contesting these seats was to receive publicity. Brian Walker's campaign in Collaroy was particularly effective because he had resigned from the Liberal Party in protest against the Government's lack of response to the widespread support of Liberal Party members for protecting the Colong Caves and Boyd Plateau.

It was clearly realised, from the inception of the campaign, that the problem was a political one and only the State Government could revoke the leases. Labor support for the preservation of Kanangra-Boyd was evident early in the campaign. In the Parliamentary debate on the National Parks and Wildlife (Amendment) Bill in November 1969, which occupied 67 pages of Hansard, much of the controversy centred on the Colong-Boyd issues. The Labor Opposition moved a motion that would amend the Bill to provide for: the cancellation of the Colong mining lease; incorporation of the area within the Kanangra-Boyd National Park; and the inclusion of the Boyd Plateau in the Park. Although the Colong Committee had approached the Premier and the Opposition for a non-party debate, both refused. The vote was therefore on strictly party lines and the amendment was defeated, although a number of Government backbenchers had expressed the hope that both areas could be included in the Park. In May 1970 the Deputy Leader of the State Opposition, Sid Einfeld, assured the Colong Committee that the Labor Party would revoke the Colong leases. The Party Leader, Pat Hills, confirmed this in a statement issued on 16 July 1970 which concluded that: 'While mining of alternative deposits of limestone may be more costly, the Labor Party believes that the preservation of the area for future generations is more important than short term profits'.

The first issue of the *Colong Bulletin*, published on 16 August 1968, contained the news that the governing body of the Liberal Party State Council had unanimously carried another resolution opposing quarrying at Colong. The resolution protested 'in the strongest possible terms' against the proposal to mine Colong and requested State Cabinet to withdraw the lease and restore the area to the proposed Kanangra-Boyd National Park. Premier Askin stated a few days later that the Government was in duty bound to reconsider the leases. On 13 September 1969 the Annual Convention of the NSW Liberal Party unanimously carried the resolution 'That this Convention urges the Askin Government to cancel limestone leases in the Colong Caves Reserve and restore the area to the Kanangra-Boyd National Park'. The resolution was applauded by delegates.

On 17 October 1969 the Sydney University Liberal Club unanimously passed a resolution calling on the Premier to revoke the mining leases. Several Liberal members of Parliament openly supported the Colong Committee, particularly Mr Max Ruddock, member for the Hills District. Two members of the Colong Committee, Mark Weatherley and Elizabeth Elenius, who were also members of the Liberal Party, framed, with Max Ruddock's guidance, resolutions which came before the State Council on 19 June 1970. The motions were not put to the Council, but a committee was established to study all available facts and to visit the areas in question in company with the relevant ministers. The site inspection, which took place on 6 and 7 September 1970 was attended not only by 15

Bent Hook Swamp on the Bindook Highlands, Blue Mountains National Park.

members of the State Council (including John Howard) but by three Ministers, Messrs Lewis (Lands), Fife (Mines) and Beale (Conservation). Also present were senior public servants from five departments – four from the National Parks and Wildlife Service, including the Director and Assistant Director; seven from the Forestry Commission, including the Deputy Chief of the Division of Forest Management; four from the Department of Mines, including the Secretary to the Minister, two Assistant Under Secretaries and the Chief Inspector of Mines; and the Director and a geologist from the Geological Survey of NSW. The size of the inspection party and the seniority of its personnel reflected the effectiveness of the Colong-Boyd campaign and the zeal of its Liberal Party protagonists.

The party inspected both the Boyd Plateau and Mount Armour, fortunately in warm, clear, early spring weather – too warm for one member who nearly passed out climbing Mount Armour. A belligerent demonstration planned by cavers and bushwalkers was fortunately converted, by the efforts of the Colong Committee, to a simple and civil proof of the presence of caves at Mount Armour.

The party dined together on the Saturday night. By this time its members thoroughly appreciated the difference between natural eucalypt forests and pine plantations and the breathtaking nature of the country which was to become a quarry site. There was vigorous debate with Ministers and expert advisers, but the focus of attention was now not whether Kanangra-Boyd could be saved but how. This was the turning point of the campaign. As Lewis left the discussion he was heard to say, 'That was worse than a Cabinet meeting'.

In November 1970 the *Australian Liberal* published the report of the State Council Committee. Inevitably the report called for 'balanced development', but it did recommend that the lease should remain 'only if no alternative deposits of limestone were determined and that 80% of the Konangaroo State Forest should remain as native forest'.

Since the Liberal Party believes that it should be responsible not to the party organisation but directly to the people, it is not therefore bound by resolutions of the organisation. There was, however, no doubt what the people, represented by both the Labor Party and the Liberal Party, wanted. Only the cement company wanted the lease to continue. The General Secretary of the NSW Division of the Liberal Party, J.L. (later Sir John) Carrick, suggested that the Labor Party was using the Colong Committee to get the Liberal Party out of office. Perhaps he was right. The tortoise-like behaviour of the Askin Government, described in the *Colong Bulletin* as 'the juggernaut Government', probably contributed to the Government's defeat in 1975.

All Parliamentarians were sent copies of the *Colong Bulletin* and asked to write to Messrs Askin, Fife, Lewis and Beale. Many questions, prompted by the Colong Committee, were asked in the House. Many Labor members supported Colong Committee policy and considerable parts of the *Colong Bulletin* were incorporated in Hansard. A slide show was attended by 29 members. When Mr Roy McCartney MP moved a motion of urgency calling for the revocation of mining leases, several hundred Colong supporters arrived at Parliament House. Prior to the 1971 election, questionnaires on environmental matters, designed for supporters to send to candidates, were sent out with the *Colong Bulletin* where it was suggested that conservation societies could prepare and publish an evaluation of candidates from a conservation viewpoint. 'How many more Colongs and Boyd Plateaus', the Bulletin asked, 'will this State suffer if we neglect the political aspect of our responsibilities as conservationists?'

Although petitions may be of limited value in themselves, some of those organised by Colong supporters attracted considerable publicity and were therefore very effective. Sydney University Nature Conservation Society organised a petition with 8,000 signatures, and petitions from 150 Catholic priests and 192 doctors were also presented to State Parliament during October 1969.

The Metropolitan Portland Cement Company was a subsidiary of Associated Portland Cement Manufacturers Ltd (APCM) – 74% of whose shares were owned by the world's largest cement company, Blue Circle Cement, which had its head office in London. Pressure was therefore exerted on

The High Gangerang from Kanangra Tops.

both APCM and Blue Circle. *Colong Bulletin No.1* carried the following report which described the attitude of the companies:

> A supporter of our cause, business executive Jim Somerville, took the trouble when in London recently to obtain an interview with some of Blue Circle's top brass. He tried to put our case across. He was met with condescension and paternalism. The Blue Circle Group have met and overcome (they say) opposition from conservationists in many parts of the world and are convinced that this 'hysterical emotionalism' will be overcome here too.

The first meeting between the Colong Committee and company representatives took place on 24 June 1969. By this time, the campaign had softened the company's attitude to the extent that it was prepared to expand its operations at Marulan in preference to mining Colong, if its investigations proved the deposits there were satisfactory. At the next meeting, in November 1970, the company reiterated this policy.

In other correspondence, the company claimed that NSW was very short of limestone, and that the use of Colong limestone 'would lower our costs and enable us to compete in Sydney with seaborne cement that is coming in at the rate of over 100,000 tons a year from Tasmania'. The *Colong Bulletin* pointed out that the only shortage of limestone in NSW was within 35 miles [58 km] of Maldon.

The limestone formations of Mt Armour were to be converted into cement.

Kanangra Gorge. The Thurat Spires on the left, Mt Cloudmaker on the far horizon.

The sale of single shares in APCM was an original and very effective tactic devised by the Colong Committee. The scheme not only elicited a great deal of attention, usually good-humoured and sympathetic, from the press, but also brought great pressure on the company. Marketable parcels of 100 shares were bought, which were then transferred, without the services of a broker, at the market price, to individual supporters. Over 1,200 shares were transferred. The possession of a single share entitled the holder to receive a copy of the annual report, a dividend, and to attend and vote at the annual general meeting, or appoint a proxy to do so. By 16 April 1969, the date of the APCM annual general meeting, there were over 200 holders of single shares, more than half of whom, or their proxies, attended the meeting. Placards were displayed outside the meeting, with such slogans as 'Colong Caves. Dedicated 1899, Dedicated 1928, Dedicated 1939, Desecrated?'

At the meeting, David Eden moved: 'That the Balance Sheet and Profit and Loss Account be received and adopted, but in view of the fact of the company's declining profitability, it reconsider its decision to mine Colong Caves because: The company's previous investigations of limestone near its Maldon works is not now "comprehensive" and it may suffer a loss of trade due to the growing unpopularity of its mining intentions'.

While the motion was defeated by 18,808,142 votes to 88, company management did agree to meet representatives of the Colong Committee to review the necessity to operate the special leases and to communicate with any groups who had information in respect to the nearby limestone deposits. The annual general meeting of 1970 was another uproarious meeting attended by even more conservationists. The main point stressed was that there was no information on the progress of the survey of alternative deposits of limestone.

The 1971 annual general meeting was held in Melbourne in order to escape the conservationists. However, four members of the Colong Committee and seven other conservationists travelled to Melbourne and were met by Laurence Rentoul who had arranged for some 200 proxy holders to attend the meeting. Intense media interest was aroused by various means, including an abseil down APCM's Melbourne office.

At the meeting Milo Dunphy moved three motions of no confidence which were ignored by the Chairman, although not by the shareholders or the press. These and other motions were lost, but one victory was gained. Terry Stern, a Sydney solicitor, challenged on the ground of insufficient notice a special resolution which would have made the minimum shareholding 20 instead of one. The Chairman said that the notice was adequate, but rather than face a threatened action in the Equity Court, which would have invalidated all the resolutions passed at the meeting, he admitted two days later that notice had been inadequate. Single share sales could therefore proceed.

By holding the meeting in Melbourne, the company had presented the Colong Committee with a publicity bonanza. In the Melbourne *Age* John Larkin wrote:

> The whole game is played according to the rules of the system, but by behaving as heavily as one of its bulldozers, as relentlessly, the company has shown the weakness of the system. When a system is so tight, so hardened, that it cannot consider, cannot accept, cannot cope with other peoples' points of view, when it pretends they do not exist, it begins to become unreal. It is out of step with the times and the more force it uses to push its way, the more resistance will come back to it. It becomes self-destructive.

In the following year (1972) the annual general meeting was held in the Mosman Town Hall. For three hours the Company's directors sat silent on the Town Hall stage while a crowd of more than 200 proxy and one-share Company shareholders harangued them for their environmental sins of the past year. To the first motion of the meeting, Milo Dunphy moved an amendment which sought relinquishment of the Colong lease and abandonment of plans for the extension of mining on the rim of Bungonia Gorge. Voting on the amendment revealed a rather neat ploy by the Company. Proxies could

Ferns and Coachwood trees (Ceratopetalum apetalum) *in a rocky rainforest gully.*

not vote on a show of hands (true, since proxies can only vote on a poll). A blue-circled card had been issued for the purpose to those shareholders present. After an uproar by conservationists objecting to a vote by this means, and a rush by them to get their cards, 200 blue-circled cards carried the amendment. The Chairman then demanded a poll, which resulted in it being defeated by over 18 million votes.

Many architects advised their clients not to use APCM cement. This was consistent with the viewpoint of the NSW Chapter of the Royal Institute of Architects, though it had not advised members of this stance. Two local councils took action on the use of APCM cement. Warringah Council refused to use it and the Ku-ring-gai Council told the Company it would 'have regard' to the Company's future actions in the Colong dispute.

Winning public support was essential for the success of the campaign. Media attention was gained by a number of activities which were reported. The most successful was the stacking of APCM meetings but many others were very effective. These included a 230 kilometre protest run from Colong Caves to Parliament House, a week-long 'cave-in' protest and abseils from the State Office Block, Central Railway Clocktower and other city buildings.

Eventually the Company undertook to relinquish the lease if satisfactory alternate deposits were available. Alternative deposits were found, not in the 300 limestone deposits elsewhere in the State, but in another reserve. Thus 'balanced development', the cosmetic of the anti-conservationists and the recommendation of the State Liberal Party sub-committee, was achieved. Three reserves, which protected some 40 hectares and extended from the edge of the limestone quarry to Bungonia Creek, were revoked. This enabled the extension of the quarry 30 metres towards Bungonia Gorge, contrary to the recommendation of the mining warden. The Colong Committee was prepared to accept the Marulan solution, provided the compromise proposed by Dr Branagan for deeper quarrying rather than extension towards the Gorge was accepted. The rejection of this solution and the extension of the quarry to the edge of the Gorge meant that Bungonia Gorge, already damaged by spill from the quarry, suffered much increased damage from rubble spillage. The Gorge is now littered with debris.

The Church Creek mining leases were revoked and added to the Kanangra-Boyd National Park on 22 March 1974.

Mountain Gum (Eucalyptus dalrympleana) *is located on undulating country above 800 metres.*

CHAPTER 4
The Boyd Campaign

THE Boyd Plateau is situated 36 km south-southwest of Katoomba, in what is now the Kanangra-Boyd National Park. It is 1,200 metres above sea level, rising in places to over 1,300 metres, which is 300 metres higher than the Blue Mountain towns. By 1970, most uplands suitable for grazing or pine plantations had been cleared. The Plateau is different from the rest of the Blue Mountains in that it is a granite dome – the eastern extension of the Bathurst Batholith. Ground cover consists of grass, unlike the sandstone country to the north, where a shrub understorey inhibits the growth of grass. It therefore provides ample feed for native fauna. Below the plateau there is a series of high waterfalls and canyons, dropping into some of the deepest gorges of the continent. The Plateau is bounded on the west by the Kowmung River and extends north to the vicinity of Jenolan Caves. The edge of the Plateau affords panoramic views, north to the central mountains, east to the Cumberland Plain and south to beyond Mittagong. At the south-eastern end of the Plateau, an outlier of Permian sandstone gives rise to Kanangra Walls, which provide a comprehensive view of the Blue Mountains. From the Walls the entire cliff line of the Blue Mountains escarpment can be viewed. The Plateau is the highest part of the Kanangra-Boyd Wilderness, one of the most scenic wilderness areas in NSW. It is less than 200 km by road from the Sydney CBD.

The scenic potential of the Boyd was recognised at the end of the 19th century, when a series of small public reserves was dedicated. In 1937, the 23,288 hectare reserve (No. 67062), for the preservation of native flora and fauna, was declared over the whole of the southern and eastern portions of the Boyd.

As soon as the road to Kanangra Walls was completed in 1940, local timber interests commenced logging in the area. The Konangaroo State Forest, in the centre of the Plateau, had been declared in 1922, but logging extended across the whole Plateau, wherever sizeable trees could be found. A National Parks Association pamphlet on the proposed Kanangra-Boyd National Park revealed a poorly concealed determination on the part of the Forestry Commission, since before 1957, to usurp R67062. On 30 December 1958, the Under Secretary of the Department of Conservation advised that the local staff of the Commission had 'overlooked the fact that the particular area was part of R67062', and, as a result, logging operations in the adjoining Konangaroo State Forest had extended into the Reserve on several occasions since 1953. The letter also stated that a road constructed by the Commission in the same Reserve 'was done without knowledge of the existence of the Reserve'. On 28 January 1958, the Under Secretary stated that the areas of the Boyd Plateau were desired by the Commission 'for the production of hardwood timber and by reason of their underlying topography and good timber cover they have little, if any, scenic recreation value'. On 10 December 1960, the Department of Lands advised the National Parks Association that the Forestry Commission had been requested to refrain from removing timber from any part of the proposed park outside the boundaries of the existing State Forest. The National Parks Association opposed the view that the Boyd Plateau 'had little or no scenic value'. The Boyd Plateau, the Association said, was essential to the Park, being the only 4,000 ft [1,200 m] granite plateau which could be reserved between Kosciuszko and New England, and having many snow-hardy floral associations deserving of national park reservation. It was used for recreation purposes by thousands of bushwalkers and Scouts each year.

Both the Minister for Lands and the Minister for Conservation refused to receive a deputation from the Association. A joint inspection by representatives of the Lands Department and the Forestry

View from Kanangra Tops towards the Wild Dog Mountains.

Commission was made while the area was blanketed in fog. Unable to see more than 20 metres, the party retired to the fireside of Jenolan Caves House, where the Forestry representatives were able to negotiate the right to log virtually the whole of the Tableland from the Lands Department whose officers had never really seen it.

Representations by the National Parks Association and the Colong Committee at the joint inspection did succeed in having 1,400 hectares, containing Dungalla Cascades and a considerable length of the Boyd Creek catchment, added to the National Park, although the latter area was savagely logged.

The Forestry Commission planned 60,000 hectares of merchantable softwood plantation. The acreage was for the purpose of establishing a pulp and paper plant, a particleboard plant and two large sawmills. For this, a huge supply of water was required and a vast amount of effluent would flow, via the Fish River, into the Macquarie River, thence through Bathurst, 50 km away, and then into the Burrendong Dam. As in other departmental proposals to use potential natural parklands, no attempt was made to investigate alternative areas. The only concession the Commission was prepared to make was the provision of 'buffer' or cosmetic strips of native forest on the edges of the Kanangra Road.

The case against the Forestry Commission's plan to establish a pine plantation on the Plateau was well expressed by Mr Coates, Independent MP for the Blue Mountains, during a debate on the National Parks and Wildlife (Amendment) Bill in November 1969. He said:

> I think it is reasonable for me to point out so as to indicate that I have some knowledge of the subject and of the bushland in question, that I was born a few miles from Jenolan Caves. I have lived in the area for the whole of my life. A large part of the area is land over which I have walked and on which I have actually logged for a considerable number of years. It is my opinion that a substantial area of land is available without the need to plant pines on the Boyd Plateau location. The area is in my view part of the Kanangra Walls system, one of the most beautiful spots in New South Wales. I hope that the regulations which are going to be given to the Company and the Government will provide some solution to eliminate the necessity for mining Colong to proceed. No doubt at a later stage submissions will be made by someone, or perhaps by myself, with regard to pine tree planting and an attempt will be made to include the Boyd Plateau in the National Park.

Regardless of such statements, the Government, on 30 January 1970, announced the addition of 9,000 hectares of the Boyd to the Konangaroo State Forest.

The NSW Government, aware of the depletion of forests, had created the Forestry Commission in 1915. The *Forestry Act* of 1916 prescribed that the Commission should 'conserve and utilise' timber, although timber that is utilised cannot be conserved, but by limiting the cut to a quota of mature trees a properly managed forest might yield timber indefinitely, and in the old days such 'sustained yield' was the aim. The Commission was further required 'to encourage the use of timber' and to 'provide' timber. There was no provision in the Act for 'utilisation', 'encouragement of use' and 'provision' to be subject to the maintenance of sustained yield, or for the preservation of forests for their ecological, scenic or recreational value. Nevertheless, the Commission might have stayed with sustained yield were it not for pressure from industry, which sought to sell rather than conserve, and was supported by the Government. In 1967, the overcutting of forests was acknowledged by a Select Committee of the Legislative Assembly, which reported that 'throughout the State unexploited or inaccessible forest areas are being roaded and logged, but at the same time areas of traditional supply are being exhausted'.

Foreseeing the inevitable decline in the output of timber from native forests, the Forestry Commission sought other means of augmenting supply. Although some eucalypts are amongst the fastest growing and tallest trees in the world, they do not mature as quickly as imported pines such as *pinus insignis* and *pinus radiata,* which are easy to plant, raise and thin for pulpwood and particle board.

Manna Gum (Eucalyptus viminalis) *occurs on basalt caps and on moist but well-drained soils in sheltered mountain valleys.*

They have the added advantage of being softwoods, in which Australian forests are deficient. Had pines been planted on derelict or eroded farmlands, they could have saved these lands from further deterioration, but instead native forests were cleared to make way for the pines. The best location for pines is uplands in high rainfall areas, and by 1970 most such lands suitable for forestry operations had been cleared and planted. The Boyd was one of the few extensive areas of open sub-alpine forest remaining and was readily available. It was then that the Commission decided to bulldoze the Plateau for a pine plantation. Mr Cocks, Secretary of the Commission, said in a letter to the Colong Committee that the Commission was 'the appropriate body to determine the future of the area'.

The Colong Committee, a little over a year from its appointment, commenced a full-scale campaign for the preservation of the forests of the Boyd Plateau. Once again a reserve was being abandoned when it became profitable for it to be desecrated. At the second meeting of supporting societies, held in March 1970, Milo Dunphy moved that:

> This meeting of representatives of the 90 public bodies supporting the aims and actions of the Colong Committee believes both the Colong Caves and the Boyd Tableland to be essential parts of the Kanangra-Boyd National Park. It deplores the actions and the principles of the NSW Government in usurping existing public reserves and Crown Lands at Mt Armour and on the Boyd for the use, in each case, of a single private company. It denounces the Government's action in gazetting 15,000 acres [6,000 hectares] of the Boyd Plateau for logging despite widespread public representations in favour of incorporating the whole of the Boyd within the National Park. It condemns the Government's persistent failure to revoke Special Lease No. 444 at Mount Armour which is the focal point of the National Park and which Associated Portland Cement Company (Aust.) is legally entitled to mine at any time.

The native forests of the Boyd Plateau were to be felled and replaced with a vast plantation of exotic pine trees.

View from Colboyd Range across the Kowmung Gorge to the Tonalli Range on the left horizon.

Mark Weatherley then moved:

> That this meeting directs the Colong Committee to extend its existing terms of reference to include a campaign to add the whole of the Boyd Plateau to the Kanangra-Boyd National Park.

Both motions were carried unanimously. For the next two years campaigns for both Colong and the Boyd were waged simultaneously. Both were in a sense 'last ditch' efforts because they involved the revocation of longstanding reserves that were immediately imperilled by development. From 1974, after the Colong lease had been surrendered, virtually the sole objective of the Colong Committee was saving the Boyd.

The Boyd campaign was a campaign against the NSW Forestry Commission, not the Government, because, like the Hydro-Electricity Commission in Tasmania, the Commission held an entrenched view that determined policy. There was no likelihood that it would reverse its policy of putting timber production and consumption before conservation, so it was necessary to persuade the State Government to override the Commission. No effective challenge had previously been directed against the clearing of native timber to make way for pine plantations. The Colong Committee, a voluntary organisation which could not match the resources of the Commission and the timber industry, and was inexperienced in political lobbying, had to devise its own methods of combating the entrenched policy. The means of doing so were similar to those adopted in the Colong Caves campaign.

The attempt to persuade the Liberal State Government to override the Commission was facilitated by Colong Committee members who belonged to Liberal Party branches. Mark Weatherley, Elizabeth Elenius and Brian Walker persuaded the State Council of the Party to appoint a Committee to report on Colong Caves and the Boyd. The Committee's report did not recommend adding Colong Caves or Konangaroo State Forest to the Kanangra-Boyd National Park – an outcome which fell far short of the Party's unanimous decision of its Annual Convention to call for the cancellation of the Colong lease. The Committee did recommend some additions to the park and the development of the State Forest in the proportion of 80% native forest and 20% softwood, and expressed appreciation of the 'pressing interest of conservation'. It recommended that the Party 'must interpret accurately the current attitudes of the electors if we are to continue to merit political leadership' and it asked 'what are the new generation thinking? Certain it is that the goals of the 1970s must differ considerably from those which gave the Liberal Party its upsurge in strength in 1949'. This statement, along with the time and attention devoted to the Colong and Boyd issues, was a credit to the Party, even though it went only part way towards the preservation of Kanangra-Boyd.

The campaign received strong support in Parliament from a number of members on both sides of the House. Support was strongest from the Labor Party, but a number of Liberal Party members were sympathetic and spoke at every opportunity. Consequently, the Boyd was never out of Parliamentary consciousness and occupied a great deal of debating time.

A lengthy debate on Colong and the Boyd took place in November 1969 on the second reading of the National Parks and Wildlife (Amendment) Bill which provided for the dedication of Kanangra-Boyd National Park. Neither Colong nor the Boyd was included in the Bill creating the proposed park, and an amendment was put forward by the Labor Party to redress the omission. Mr George Petersen made a far-seeing speech in which he recognised the emergence of conservation as a major political issue. He said:

> I do not think it is readily appreciated by many honourable members that a new dimension of politics has come up recently, people are not concerned with economic issues only, they are concerned with what is called broadly the quality of life. We are not willing to accept the old North Country slogan 'muck means brass'. We reject it. The quality of life is important as well as the economics. It is important that we have

A deep pool in the Bulga Denis Canyon, Kowmung River, Kanangra-Boyd National Park.

aesthetic values incorporated in our lives. It is significant that a new group of people are arriving who are not just content to accept the dictates of State and Commonwealth bureaucracy, who are not content to accept what are represented to them as economic imperatives.

On 5 March 1970, after a visit to the Boyd with Colong Committee members, Mr Petersen said that the planned pine plantation would create an ecological desert in the heart of an important wilderness area and he criticised the Government for creating national parks only in areas of no economic value. The next day he attempted, for the second time, to raise the issue as a matter of urgency, describing the newly constructed roads in the forest 'which made it obvious that the Forestry Commission intends to remove every stick of native timber from the Plateau'. He said that there were 1.8 million hectares of land suitable for pine plantations in the State. Land elsewhere might cost a million dollars, but: 'What is the value of a national park?' The Forestry Commission 'was obviously determined to destroy the last decent sub-alpine forest in central NSW'.

In the Legislative Council, the Leader of the Opposition moved an amendment on similar lines to that moved in the Assembly and was defeated, though the Minister for Decentralisation and Development, the Hon. John Fuller, referred to a 'guarantee' that the Colong lease would be exchanged if suitable alternative deposits were found. The finding of alternatives was left, as usual, to the conservationists. The Bill did add 2,500 hectares of R67062 to the Park. The area had been heavily logged in accord with the Forestry Commission's unwritten policy of logging proposed parks before they were dedicated. The adjoining Konangaroo State Forest was unlogged.

Because the pine planting program was funded by the Federal Government, the Colong Committee was able to bring the issue into national focus. Senator Cotton, Minister for Civil Aviation,

The Thurat Spires on the western edge of Kanangra Gorge. The Thurat Range, seen on the far horizon, could have been planted with pines.

was a director of Timber Industries Ltd, the logging company operating on the Boyd, in which the Cotton family held a 43% interest. On 12 April 1970, Mr Al Grassby raised the subject in Federal Parliament. He asked the Minister for National Development, Mr Reginald Swartz, to appeal to Senator Cotton to halt the Timber Industries 'savage logging operations on the Boyd Tableland'.

In August 1972, Colong Committee member Mr Neil Mackerras, an official of the Democratic Labor Party, acting upon the advice of the Committee, interviewed Senator Kane (DLP) and suggested an amendment to the Softwoods Forestry Agreements Bill. The amendment would add the word 'environmental' to clause 9, which would then read 'the State shall ensure that planting each year is carried out efficiently and in accord with sound forestry, environmental and financial practices'. The amendment also proposed a new clause to read: 'The State will ensure that natural forests shall not be cleared for planting softwoods unless the particular proposed clearing has beforehand been the subject of an environmental impact study made by an independent expert on behalf of the Australian Forestry Council and that the Council, after considering the report of the said study, has approved the particular clearing'. Senator Cotton, who was Leader of the Government in the Senate, tried to dissuade Senator Kane from moving the amendment, but Senator Kane would not do so and the Bill was deferred to the next session. The Bill was introduced on 19 April 1972. Mr Tom Uren, who spoke for 1 hour and 22 minutes, described the Bill as 'a classic case of national development designed and financed on the narrowest of economic considerations and based on very speculative future projections of Australia's future population and per capita consumption of wood. The Bill contains not one word of the large environmental impact of the policies contained in it'. The Bill was debated in the Senate on 14 August when Senator Kane's amendment was carried and the Bill returned to the House of Representatives, where it was not accepted. In its place, an amendment was made which stated that 'in the schedule, at the end of clause 9, add "and shall ensure that environmental factors relating to the planting have been considered"'. The provision for an environmental impact study by the Australian Forestry Council was therefore removed, leaving the Forestry Commission to be the judge of its own cause.

As the previous softwood plantation agreement had expired on 30 June 1971, millions of conifers had been growing on credit for over 15 months. The environment rated well below forestry and finance, both of which had to be based on 'sound' principles. The environmental principles apparently didn't need to be sound and the environment had merely to be 'considered'.

The Colong Committee leaflet, 'Park or Pines', and other papers supplied by the Committee, provided the backbone of the Parliamentary debate and were incorporated in various speeches. The Prime Minister, Mr Gough Whitlam, told a press conference that the Parliamentary Party had discussed the Bill no less than five times. He said that the Boyd had occupied more Caucus time during the year than any other issue. Although not written specifically for the Boyd, a paper entitled 'The Pine Planting Program in NSW – an exercise in environmental irresponsibility', by R. and V. Routley of the Australian National University, exposed the Forestry Commission's expanded estimate of the land required for pine plantations from 0.6 million hectares in 1960 to 1.8 million hectares in 1972. The expansion was a promotional plea, based on exaggerated population growth estimates and the addition of timber exports to domestic needs. 'Planners', the paper stated, 'are committed to the belief that it is their business to attempt to raise the consumption of wood products'. High American consumption was due to increased packaging and leaflet and newspaper advertising, 'a type and level of consumption which was unnecessary, environmentally damaging, and making only a very doubtful contribution to increasing the standard of living'. The forestry planners had taken it upon themselves to decide that 'a satisfying and diverse environment is less important than more cardboard boxes, excessive packaging and throwaway paper products'. No allowance was made for the podsolisation and exhaustion of soil nutrients which were a feature of coniferous plantations, and even under the common assumption of foresters that the land they used had no value for any other purpose, and that there were no administrative costs and land rates, the rate of return was below prevailing returns in other forms of investment.

The Laurie, Montgomery and Petit Report, published in May 1972, was entitled 'Draft Investigation of Validity of Preliminary Guidelines for Assessment of Environmental Impact Study for Afforestation Project at Konangaroo State Forest No 750'. *Colong Bulletin No. 33* described it as a 'report on a plan for reporting on a report on a plan'. The paper did show evidence that the authors had read 'Park or Pines' and the Routley paper. It questioned the rationality of the Forestry Commission's plans to produce, by the turn of the century, 15 times the volume of softwoods then harvested, and recommended upgraded silvicultural practices to produce more hardwoods.

As a means of effectively presenting its case, the Colong Committee prepared a photographic display book featuring photographs by Henry Gold. The hard-hitting text was written by Peter Manning, then Executive Producer of the ABC's *4 Corners* television program, and Kaj Elenius provided

Box Creek originates on the Boyd Plateau and drops with numerous falls and cascades into the Kowmung River below. Logging the plateau would have choked this creek with silt.

The Thurat Walls above the Kanangra Deep.

the diagrams. Together with mounting, printing, assembly and binding, the book cost about $1,000. On 1 March 1974, the State Pollution Control Commission (SPPC) advertised 'an environmental investigation of a proposal for pine planting on the Boyd'. Mr Freudenstein, had succeeded Mr Beale as Minister for Conservation because, according the *Sydney Morning Herald*, Mr Beale's handling of the Boyd had already prejudged the result of the investigation. The decision to conduct an investigation fell far short of the Colong Committee's demand for an environmental impact study. However, after discussion with members of the Committee, Mr Eric Coffey, Director of the SPCC, agreed that the Forestry Commission report was inadequate and requested further information from the Commission.

The investigation proved both thorough and impartial. Ninety submissions were made. One of the most important came from the National Trust, largely written by Denise Black, who had written a thesis on the Boyd Plateau and spent months there identifying species. Colong's book on the area proved very effective in the Inquiry, providing a vicarious visit to the Plateau for the commissioners, who seemed unable to take a four-hour drive to personally inspect an area the future of which they were debating.

The Forestry Commission's claims were rejected and the Colong Committee's reasoning that parklands could not be assessed in economic terms accepted. The SPCC's report said that the Forestry Commission's estimate of up to $2 million for purchase of land 'would need to be assessed against the worth to the community of preserving the Boyd Plateau in its natural state. This is a subjective judgment which is not capable of measurement in monetary terms. Having regard to the likely order of accuracy of the Commission's assessment of the area necessary for a hypothetical pulp mill (40,000 acres [16,000 hectares], increased to 60,000 acres [24,000 hectares] during the Boyd campaign) the area of 4,000 to 5,000

View to the north from Roaring Wind Mountain across the Kowmung Valley with Boyd Plateau on the left. Crafts Wall is the prominent flat-topped mountain in the background.

The roots of a fig tree cling to rocks in a fern gully.

acres [1,600–2,000 hectares] available on the Boyd Plateau was not considered critical'. The Committee's submission on scientific values, regeneration of native vegetation, animal habitat, amenity value and wilderness quality was endorsed and the SPCC's recommendations were concise and to the point. They were:

> The pine planting should not proceed within the Konangaroo State Forest on the Boyd Plateau. The further damage to the natural environment within the Konangaroo State Forest should not be permitted, except to the extent that it is necessary to assist positive enjoyment of the area by the public… The Commission sees the recommendation as being consistent with other steps taken to protect the environment of the Blue Mountains, such as the rejection of the proposal to construct a natural gas pipe line across the Blue Mountains and the voluntary surrender of limestone mining at Mount Armour on the south-eastern boundary of the Kanangra-Boyd National Park, approximately 14 kilometres from the Boyd Plateau.

In January 1975 the Forestry Commission completed an 'Environmental Investigation of Pine Planting in the Konangaroo State Forest', which the Commission described as an Environmental Impact Statement and the Colong Committee described as 'The 10.7% Report' – 10.7% was the estimated rate of return from the pine plantation, achieved by ignoring land value and alternative land uses. Nor was destruction of native flora and fauna assessed. There was no indication where roads would go, what sensitive areas would be reserved, nor any study by a zoologist, hydrologist, soil scientist or botanist.

On 13 April 1975, immediately after the publication of the report and findings of the SPCC investigation, the Minister for Lands and Forests, the Hon. Milton Morris, announced that there would be no planting of pines on the Boyd. This ended the seven-year campaign.

The environmental result of establishing a pine plantation on the Boyd was simple and obvious. The entire native flora and fauna dependent on it would have been destroyed, with a very limited range of species possibly returning in time. Had the Forestry Commission acknowledged this fact, and the fact that parkland could not be valued in dollars, it would have made a considerable saving. It is probable that the value of staff time engaged on publicity, report compilation, letter writing, etc. and overheads, together with the cost of clearing the Boyd, exceeded the cost of buying 3,000 hectares of grazing land.

The saving of the Kanangra-Boyd Wilderness was a landmark in nature conservation. It is one of the largest and most scenic areas in the state and for the first time the clearing of native forest for pine planting had been stopped. The Konangaroo State Forest was added to the Kanangra-Boyd National Park on 8 July 1977.

A stand of Coachwoods in warm temperate rainforest.

CHAPTER 5

Wollemi, and the Colo

by Haydn Washington

THE path to World Heritage listing for the Colo-Hunter Wilderness was long and involved. Members of the Colo Committee speak of the Colo-Hunter Wilderness, because for them it was never 'Wollemi'. Wollemi was just a big creek that joined the Colo River. During the whole campaign the focus was the Colo River, that 'Grand Canyon' of NSW – the longest sandstone gorge in the state. The Colo Committee took a thousand people to visit the Colo during the campaign – they never took anyone to Wollemi Creek! The name Wollemi came later, for political reasons.

The Colo-Hunter Wilderness, or Northern Blue Mountains, is one of those areas that was in large part 'forgotten' until the mid-1970s. In the south, Bells Line of Road had gone through in early days, cutting the Colo River system off from the Grose River catchment. And the Lower Colo River valley was cleared early on. Development of the western plains continued throughout the 1800s, up to the sandstone escarpment and mountains of the edge of the northern Blue Mountains. The northern area was developed along the Widden Brook and Goulburn River around the same period, due to good water, easier gradients and alluvial soils. The Colo Wilderness was not completely cut off from the Macdonald (Yengo) Wilderness in the east until the Second World War, when the Putty Road was finally upgraded from Putty, a grazing enclave, to the Hunter Valley. The road was only sealed in the 1960s.

All attempts to find a suitable route along the Colo Gorge in the south, from east to west, failed. There was little good grazing or timber country and no accessible minerals in most of the area. In 1883 the gorge defied attempts by George Townshend, an employee of the Works Department, to survey a passable railway line. Similarly, at the turn of the century, it defied the shale miners to survey an oil pipeline. There was also a proposal in 1901 by The Electric Company for a hydro-electric scheme near Tootie Creek junction, with a dam 90 metres high that would have formed a lake 35 km long and produced '12,000 horsepower of electric energy'. However, the scheme failed. There was sporadic low-scale timber getting in some areas and the odd basalt cap was grazed, but otherwise the area of about 500,000 hectares was left largely as vacant Crown Land. A few bushwalkers visited the area, but as late as 1974 few had walked the Capertee-Colo Gorge from Glen Davis down to Upper Colo (a 120 km trip). Two parts of the wilderness were timber reserves, and the Coricudgy State Forest lay to the west of the area (and encompassed part of the wilderness). The Army used a central area to the north of the Capertee River for training.

Unlike most wilderness areas, this one – NSW's largest – sat on Sydney's doorstep, only 70 km from Sydney's centre. Like most wilderness areas, it had only survived as an accident of history. A proposal to develop the area in a major way came from the then Colo Shire Council (now in Hawkesbury Shire) when it commissioned a study to develop tourism in the Shire in 1974. This study proposed a number of major roads and lookouts in the wilderness along the Colo Gorge – even a bridge across the gorge was suggested. Such a bridge would have been the size of the Sydney Harbour Bridge.

At this time I became the honorary secretary of the Colo Committee. Formed initially at the instigation of Milo Dunphy of the Total Environment Centre (TEC) in Sydney, the Committee soon became independent. Its first priority was to respond to Colo Shire Council's tourism study report,

The Colo River, below its junction with Wollemi Creek, cuts a deep gorge through the sandstone plateau.

which contained many errors. The Committee started off with three biologists and two geologists, and was later to gain members with expertise in graphic art, photography, political science and accounting. Although the tourism proposal lapsed because of insufficient funds, it became obvious that, since so little was known about the area, there needed to be a new national park proposal.

Building on a park proposal previously developed by the National Parks Association of NSW (NPA), which had covered most of the area, the Colo Committee started researching the area in detail. After two years of study they submitted a new proposal to the State Government. The receptiveness of the Wran Labor Government to conservation issues was a major factor in the fight for the Colo. In 1976, a report from the Department of Geography of the University of New England, '*Wilderness in Australia*' (the 'Helman Report'), was released. This showed that the Colo-Hunter was three times the size of the State's next largest wilderness, Kanangra-Boyd, and that its core area was 235,000 hectares. From this point the Colo Committee, the Colong Foundation, Total Environment Centre and the National Parks Association urged that all of the wilderness be placed inside a national park.

Between 1976 and 1979 there was an intense period of talks to small and large groups, including schools and universities, women's discussion groups and community organisations. In 1977 the Colo Committee completed a hinged eight-panel display on the Colo, which toured various locations around Sydney, and Premier Wran visited the Southern Blue Mountains at Batsh Camp near Colong Caves. During this trip, the Colo Committee gave a copy of the Helman Report to the Premier, and he promised to meet with them. On this visit representatives of the Colo Committee also met Dick Smith, the electronics millionaire, whose help was to prove invaluable in saving the area.

Also that year the State Pollution Control Commission conducted the Culoul Range Shale Mining inquiry. The Culoul Range is the highest range on the south-east side of the Park. The range

Wolgan Valley at Rocky Creek confluence.

The hard-leaved Scribbly Gum (Eucalyptus sclerophylla) *is common on sandy soils throughout the Blue Mountains.*

runs northwest to the junction of the Colo River and Wollemi Creek. It has two shale caps, and one basalt cap. Autobric Pty Ltd proposed to mine both shale caps. The inquiry was well attended by conservation bodies which put in a sixty-two page joint submission, based on the wilderness quality of the area. It was here that the National Parks and Wildlife Service (NPWS) first publicly stated its interest in creating a large national park over the area. The NPWS stated that the Culoul Range was of major importance to the park proposal, while the company argued that the Culoul Range was environmentally 'commonplace'. The latter claim was refuted when the Colo Committee discovered Brush Turkeys on the range and the company's own consultant, Harry Recher, had to admit that this was at the time the southernmost distribution of the bird, and therefore of importance. It was also put forward that there were plentiful shale reserves elsewhere. In September, the inquiry report found insufficient reasons for mining and discussed the wilderness importance of the area.

A deputation from the Colo Committee met Premier Wran in September 1977. He was the first Premier for a number of years to meet conservationists, and much of the success that followed was due to his personal interest in the area. The Colo Committee discussed a number of threats to the area, including mining and logging, but the number one priority was the proposals by the Electricity Commission. For a number of years there had been rumours of proposals by the Commission in connection with the Colo Wilderness.

In early 1978, following rumours of a road having been built along Boorai Ridge to the cliff above the Colo, members of the Colo Committee discovered a flow metre had been installed on the Colo in the wilderness, just above Boorai Creek, along with five kilometres of new road along Boorai Ridge. The Commission had also built a helipad and cut a track down to the Colo River. Two discarded garbage bags and other refuse identified the culprit. The Colo Committee subsequently

The Yodeller Range forms part of the dramatic northern boundary of the Blue Mountains. This view from Nullo Mountain is looking north toward the Hunter Valley.

Sculptured by water, the impressive walls of this canyon narrow to a slot only a few metres wide.

gained possession of confidential minutes of a meeting that had taken place between the State Pollution Control Commission and Elcom on 3 February 1978. These spelt out plans for: a power station on Newnes Plateau; a potential dam on the Colo; and a surface easement between the dam and the power station to accommodate a water supply pipe line and a transmission line and road. Shortly thereafter the Australian Museum and the National Herbarium, amongst others, were employed as consultants on work for a possible environmental impact statement. The scheme involved a corridor cut right across the wilderness.

The lobbying campaign went into full swing. From every public meeting or talk attended, letters were sent to the Government urging that the dam be stopped and the area be declared a national park. The ABC TV program *This Day Tonight* produced a television news documentary on the wilderness and the dam, and journalists ran articles on the Colo Wilderness and the dam that threatened it.

In April 1978, Mr Crabtree (then Minister for Lands and National Parks) met with the Colo Committee and informed them that guidelines in regard to coal mining were being worked on between the NPWS and the Mines Department. He promised to raise the issue of the dam with Pat Hills, the Minister for Energy and Water Resources. Sources later informed the Committee that Mr Crabtree was considering a 'strip park' covering only the river, in order to avoid fights between departments.

In May the Colo Committee finally met with the Power Development Section of the Electricity Commission. It was obvious they thought the project would go ahead. They indicated that the Colo

In 1978, the Electricity Commission proposed the Colo Gorge, in the heart of the largest wilderness in NSW, as a dam site.

The Colo Gorge near the Capertee River junction.

was the only large scale water resource as yet uncommitted to enlarging Sydney's water supplies and that it was the cheapest to develop. They expected water to come out of the Colo in ten years, which meant construction in four to five years.

Shortly after this meeting the Colo Committee produced an item of critical importance in the campaign, which basically led to suppression of the Colo dam proposal. With the help of $4,000 from Committee member Dick Smith, the Committee published a full-page advertisement in the *Sydney Morning Herald* titled: 'Colo River – NSW's Lake Pedder?' This set out the argument for saving the area from the Electricity Commission proposals. It asked people to write letters or send an attached coupon to the Government. This resulted in around 800 letters and 4,000 coupons flooding in – the greatest public response the Government had had on a single issue for many years.

To add to the public outcry, 1978 saw the publication of two important books on the area. The first, *Colo Wilderness*, was written by Peter Prineas, director of NPA, with black and white photos by Henry Gold. The second, but less significant, was *Wilderness in Danger – a Case Study of the Northern Blue Mountains* by Michael Bell and Associates, from the Total Environment Centre.

The Colo Committee also began detailed research into the power station proposed for Newnes Plateau and it looked into alternatives. A document, 'Wilderness and Power – the Case against a Power Station on Newnes Plateau and Suggested Alternatives – with Special Reference to Heavy Metals', was published in February 1979. It suggested that if a power station was needed, it could be built at Pipers Flat, near Portland, and that coal could come from further north while water could come from Williwa Creek, a large creek polluted by the abandoned heavy metal mine of Sunny Corner. It stated that pollution of the Colo system would inevitably result from mining of the Newnes Plateau.

The Army too posed a significant threat in 1978. Troops had been training in the middle of the proposed park for a number of years. The Air Force also had a dirt airstrip near Gospers Mountain. In late 1978, the Committee discovered that the Army had plans to upgrade the existing rough Wirraba Trail to two-wheel drive standard. The Army used this area through a lease arrangement with the State Government, and some preliminary work had been started. The Colo Committee sent off an urgent telegram to the Minister for Defence. It also wrote to Mr Crabtree, who strongly objected to the renewal of the Army's lease, which had lapsed. The Army threat was laid to rest with the help of the NSW Minister for Lands, Mr Paul Landa, in early 1979.

By 1979 the dam proposal had been swamped by a flood of public opinion. The key problem was getting the park proclaimed. This was aided by a change of Minister for the Environment, from Mr Crabtree to Mr Landa. Mr Landa actually encouraged and fought for existing and proposed national parks, aided by what he described as his alter ego (and chief advisor) John Whitehouse. In 1979, the Committee worked with Channel Ten to produce a *John Laws' World* special, 'The Wilderness Sydney Forgot', an hour-long program on the Colo (which screened in 1980).

Forestry activities on the edge of the wilderness had been winding down for a number of decades, however there were still some 50 to 60 people employed in timber mills which took trees out of the proposed park. The mill owners soon mounted a campaign, which asserted that 1,000 people would be out of work if the park was created. Rumours were also circulated that all land next to the wilderness would be resumed. The Colo Committee held talks in local areas, but it proved difficult to break through the paranoia generated by those opposing wilderness protection. The Colo Committee produced a study on forestry, suggesting that forests could be taken out of the Cessnock sub-district and put into the Sydney sub-district to provide sawlogs closer to those mills.

In early 1979, Dick Smith sent all members of State Parliament a copy of the book *Colo Wilderness*. On 24 April 1979, Mr Landa opened the Second South Pacific Parks Conference at the Sydney Opera House and announced the establishment of the fiftieth national park in New South Wales – the 502,000 hectare Wollemi National Park. The Park was called 'Wollemi' after the longest

A typical sand bank of the Colo River reveals the river's everchanging water levels.

watercourse inside it, although conservationists wanted the national park to be called 'Colo' or 'Colo-Hunter'.

Mr Landa announced that the addition of the Wollemi National Park increased the area of national parks in NSW by 25 per cent, and that: 'the reservation of this magnificent new park is significant not only for NSW but for Australia and the world... Nowhere else in the world does a major city have on its doorstep a world-class national park such as Wollemi'. He continued: 'it is intended to retain the central core as a wilderness zone where people will be encouraged to undertake the hardy recreational pursuits for which this area of the park is already famous'.

However, on a less pleasant note for conservationists, Mr Landa admitted that an agreement had 'been reached to enable the exploration and underground extraction, only, of coal resources in a controlled fashion without interference with those natural values'.

The editorial of the *Sydney Morning Herald* on the following day carried the heading, 'Paradise Now'. It stated that Mr Landa had shifted attention from conventional national parks to wilderness areas, and that 'this change of emphasis is a hallmark in Australian conservation'. The editorial concluded: 'The benefits to the people of Sydney and, indeed, Australia, from the preservation of this vast wilderness surely outweigh the objections'.

The good news was that most of the wilderness core and adjoining management zone (as defined by the Helman Report) was in the park. The dam appeared to be quashed. The bad news involved the creation of the Putty State Forest, and the allowance of logging to continue for four years

A stand of hard-leaved Scribbly Gums (Eucalyptus schlerophylla) *above the Wollangambe Valley in the central Blue Mountains.*

A rocky ridge drops steeply to the Colo River below.

within the park, making the Wollemi the first such park to be logged after dedication. Further bad news was the coal mining.

Since the park had not yet been gazetted, lobbying continued. Public reaction was largely favourable. The tentative agreement on coal mining appeared in the form of a document called 'Resolution of Conflicts between Underground Extraction of Coal Resources and Dedication and Management of Areas as National Parks and Nature Reserves'. This was the basis for a 'gentleman's agreement' between Mr Landa and Mr Mulock (Minister for Mineral Resources), under which the Department of Mineral Resources withdrew objections to the park. Public criticism of the mining proposal was increasing during the latter half of 1979. Correspondence with the Premier and Mr Landa assured the Committee that gazettal would take place before Christmas. Mr Wran also accepted an invitation issued by the combined environment groups to come on a walk to the Colo at Canoe Creek in late November 1979. Although complaining that rock-hopping was really 'suicide attempting', Mr Wran did well as he walked the six kilometres and 230 metres descent to the river and back, to experience the wilderness at first hand.

On 14 December 1979, the Wollemi National Park was gazetted – 'to the centre of the Earth'. This meant that there could be no mining 'under' the park. In early 1980, a deputation of conservation bodies saw Mr Wran agree that no mining should need to take place under parks for 50 years, and that no mining would take place during his period of government. Cabinet later rejected the 'gentleman's agreement' and Wollemi National Park was given a reprieve from coal mining. At about this time the Electricity Commission announced plans to build a power station at Mt Piper, abandoning plans for a power station on Newnes Plateau, and hence a dam on the Colo River.

After all the painstaking research, all the lobbying and time spent on a major, successful campaign, it would be nice to think it had a happy ending, but twenty more laborious years were needed. Despite Wollemi being the second largest park in the State and being close to Sydney, it received no funding

Wedding Cake Mountain in the Yodeller Range, northern Blue Mountains.

The combined forces of water and wind cause an effect known locally as 'honeycomb weathering' in the sandstone.

for the first year and less than $20,000 for the following year. It had the equivalent of only two staff attached, and there were no serious moves towards a management plan for many years (even though the Colo Committee presented its own suggested draft). Indeed, the final Plan of Management was only published with the World Heritage announcement, more than two decades later.

Even with Mr Landa's assurances, no moves had been made to zone the Colo Wilderness under the *National Parks and Wildlife Act*. So the years went by and the Colo Committee wound down from an active group meeting weekly to one which, while still active, was far more sedate. In 1986, the Wilderness Working Group, established by the then Minister for the Environment Bob Carr, again found that Wollemi was the largest wilderness in NSW, with an area of around 400,000 hectares. However, the NPWS still did not gazette a Wollemi Wilderness. Finally, in 1995, the Colo Committee nominated a wilderness area under the *Wilderness Act*. The Committee proposal was larger than the 1976 Helman wilderness area, and slightly larger than the Wilderness Working Group's identified area, but did not include the whole park. The NPWS came up with a modest identified wilderness area of 288,000 hectares, of which 257,420 hectares was in Wollemi National Park. The 4WD movement ran a strong campaign opposing the wilderness nomination. In particular they wanted to keep open the Hunter Trail in the north, and thus chop the wilderness area into two sections.

Despite all the Colo Committee had fought for, all that was promised, it looked as though the Wollemi Wilderness might still not receive the protection it deserved. The Colong Foundation for Wilderness, National Parks Association, Total Environment Centre and The Wilderness Society were lobbying to expand the proposed wilderness using a document called the 'Wollemi Wilderness Plan' and a brochure which was circulated widely. Over 10,000 letters in support were collected at street stalls by the Colong Foundation, The Wilderness Society and others.

The ultimate prize of gaining World Heritage, however, was due to two things, the first being the nomination for the Greater Blue Mountains, put forward by the Colong Foundation, and the second the *Wollemia nobilis*, the Wollemi Pine. This new species was discovered in Wollemi National Park in September 1994 by David Noble. This 'pinosaur with Jurassic bark' captured the imagination of the world, as detailed in James Woodford's book *The Wollemi Pine*.

Woodford worked out the location of the pine during his extensive research for the book. At this time, Premier Bob Carr was assuring IUCN (and hence UNESCO) that the Wollemi Pine was inside the NPWS-identified wilderness. Woodford was in a position to tell him that it wasn't. The result was that 361,000 hectares were declared as the Wollemi Wilderness on 5 March 1999, an area larger than the area initially identified as wilderness and similar to that proposed by peak environment groups in the Wollemi Wilderness Plan. In fact, Wollemi is one of the few natural areas where both the national park and the wilderness area have ended up being *larger* than those initially proposed by environment groups.

The upshot is that the largest wilderness in the state, close to the continent's largest city, is now protected as wilderness. The Colo Committee's involvement with this went back 28 years, while that of other conservationists for the Blue Mountains goes back much further. At a recent celebration of World Heritage in Wollemi National Park in 2001, it was brought home to the Colo Committee just how much of the saga to save Wollemi had been forgotten, and that NSW almost lost this vast wilderness. Perhaps this chapter can serve as a reminder that a lot of work by a lot of people gave us Wollemi National Park. To keep it will require vigilance by all who love wilderness.

Wollemi Pine (Wollemia nobilis), *discovered in 1994, remains safe within the labyrinth of the Wollemi Wilderness. Photo: J Plaza. Royal Botanic Gardens, Sydney.*

CHAPTER 6

Further Additions to the Park System

WITH the reservation of the Blue Mountains, Kanangra-Boyd and Wollemi National Parks, most of the Northern, Central and Southern Divisions of Myles Dunphy's Greater Blue Mountains National Park proposal had been reserved, but not the Nattai Division further south, or the Gardens of Stone area, including Newnes Plateau on the western edge of the Blue Mountains. The protection of Nattai took a further 20 years to achieve, while protection for the Gardens of Stone remains a work in progress, with key areas such as the Airly-Genowlan Mesa still threatened by coal mining.

The Nattai, reserved in 1991, was the fourth division of Myles Dunphy's Greater Blue Mountains National Park to be fully protected. Myles initially visited the area in 1916, the first bushwalker to go there. He returned there five times between 1928 and 1931.

The campaign to save the Nattai began in the mid 1920s, when Myles somewhat naively wrote to the Forestry Commission suggesting that the tall forests of the 15 km long Couridjah Corridor be protected in a reserve for public recreation. This canyon, south-west of Picton, contains the most accessible blue gum forest anywhere near Sydney, providing walking access to this spectacular Blue Mountains canyon without the effort of a major descent from its entry point, downstream of Thirlmere Lakes. The early walkers did not know it at the time but the Couridjah Corridor, with its entrenched stream meanders, is a geological marvel. The gradual rate of uplift over millennia was equalled by the stream capacity to cut into the rock producing an extensive, meandering gorge.

Forestry interests, disregarding the proposal for a recreation reserve, lost no time establishing a sawmill crew in the Nattai, and over the next ten years the merchantable timber was removed. The logging was a serious blow to the early conservationists and an important lesson. Myles Dunphy noted 'foresters cannot bear to see a tree die, fall down and rot. But nevertheless many forms of animate forest-life depend on that natural condition'. The logging was never repeated, and over the last 70 years these forests have recovered much of their former majesty. Fortuitously, the reservation of the Warragamba Water Supply Catchment in 1942 offered a level of protection to the Nattai Division of Myles' Greater Blue Mountains National Park.

The National Trust in 1968, joined by the National Parks Association of NSW in 1974, renewed the original push for a reserve. By September 1973, coal mining had caused a very damaging 600,000 cubic metre cliff fall alongside Lake Burragorang to the north of the proposal, and development pressures were mounting. A hard rock quarry at Mount Flora, to the south, was proposed in 1976 and urban expansion had begun to leapfrog villages from Thirlmere to Hilltop. By 1984, plans were being drawn up for a Mittagong bypass over the Nattai River and a shooting range was relocated in 1986 to Wattle Ridge, within the proposed park, in order to make way for the planned road.

In October 1986, in response to these developments, the Colong Foundation for Wilderness and Total Environment Centre commissioned Keith Muir to prepare a park plan. A 75,000 hectare Nattai National Park proposal, with a 30,000 hectare wilderness core, was released in December 1987, just in time to be caught up in the election promises for the next State election, three months later. In February 1988 the proposal became the second wilderness area nominated under the *Wilderness Act, 1987*.

Endorsements for the Nattai National Park proposal were quickly secured from two leading local NSW Parliamentarians – Mr Robert Webster, the Member for Goulburn, and Mr John Fahey, Member for the Southern Highlands. These endorsements were prominently featured in a widely circulated brochure promoting the park proposal.

Red Bloodwood (Eucalyptus gummifera) *is widely distributed across the dissected plateaus and ridges of the Blue Mountains.*

Tim Moore, Environment Minister in the new Greiner Government, was keen to strengthen relationships with the NSW environment movement, and in October 1988 he joined a bushwalking inspection of the area. George Threlfo of the Blue Mountains Conservation Society led the party. It included representatives of the Water Board and conservation groups, as well as the ministerial group. They walked down bushranger Starlight's Track to McArthurs Flat on the Nattai River.

The trip was a great success, but Tim Moore was concerned that objections to the park proposal by the Department of Mineral Resources, due to underlying coal resources, would interfere with the dedication of the park. These concerns seemed misplaced, as there had been six unsuccessful attempts to establish collieries in the area. Margaret Robertson, who had been prominent in the campaign for Australia's first wilderness act only six months before, pointed out that the Nattai was one of the easiest proposals to achieve reservation, since it was nearly all Crown land, managed by the Water Board as a strictly protected water catchment area. Apparently the support of Messrs Fahey, Webster and Moore was insufficient to overcome opposition to the park within Government.

In August 1989, to maintain bipartisan support for the park, the Colong Foundation and the Berrima NPA took Ms Pam Allan, then Shadow Minister for the Environment, Madi Maclean, and Allan Hansell, Research Officer for Bob Carr, on a 4WD tour of the proposed park. John Wrigley, the Water Board's Catchment Manager, conducted the tour through the inner catchment of Lake Burragorang (Warragamba Dam). The inspection party stayed with Colong Foundation's long-term member Rosyln Badgery on her 840 hectare cattle property, situated on the Wanganderry Tableland overlooking the Nattai. Unfortunately, the two-day circumnavigation of the proposed park, mainly confined to 4WD vehicles using rough roads, caused more nausea than a sense of wonder. It was belatedly realised that support is best secured by immersion in nature, not by quick and comfortable site inspections, however thorough.

The tour confirmed the threat posed by the spectacular Mount Flora quarry site, a prominent peak now controlled by CSR-Readymix. The proposed quarry would be the most scenic in the state, with views extending over the Nattai Wilderness to the Boyd Plateau, Mount Colong to the north and, in the east, views to the city and the distinctive arch of Sydney Harbour Bridge. A major hard rock quarry was planned to replace the CSR-Readymix quarry at Prospect, but was strongly opposed by the Wingecarribee Shire Council and local residents.

The major quarry and freeway bypass proposals rallied the local Southern Highlands community behind moves to protect the Nattai area. The Colong Foundation for Wilderness and the Berrima Branch of the National Parks Association convened several well-attended public meetings to discuss the park plan, and met no opposition. A Friends of Nattai group was established to help co-ordinate the local support for the park proposal and opposition to the quarry. A number of walks were conducted to keep an eye on developments being undertaken in the area. On one walk, a line of blue tags, trees gashed with blue blazes and river stones marked in blue paint was discovered stretching the entire length of the Nattai Valley.

Enquiries revealed that a so-called Nattai Foundation, whose aim was to make a walking track from Mittagong to Katoomba, had been established. When funds for a track were not forthcoming, it had started to cut the track without council permission. This Foundation proposed 12 bridges, tree removal at camp sites, concrete and brick fireplaces, water tanks, seven huts, six radio posts and 4WD vehicle support for walkers so that packs need not be carried into the wilderness. Fortunately, neither the Wingecarribee Shire Council nor the Crown Lands Office approved the damaging project.

The Colong Foundation also spearheaded opposition to a Mt Flora quarry that would have established an open-cut mine next to the Nattai Wilderness. The quarry required the removal of a prominent mountain top and ultimately a kilometre-long pit would have been formed. Irregularities in the approval process, discovered by the Foundation, obliged CSR-Readymix to re-exhibit its proposal

Nattai River, Nattai National Park. A recent flood has exposed the roots of an old River Oak (Casuarina cunninghamiana).

for public comment. This bought valuable time, but it was neither possible to obtain the intervention of the Greiner Government nor establish a public inquiry into why a quarry at Mt Flora was necessary when another massive quarry was proposed just a few kilometres away at Mt Misery.

Inevitably, with the local Wingecarribee Shire Council opposing the project, the issue was referred to the Land and Environment Court. For three weeks in October 1990, Keith Muir, acting for the Colong Foundation, opposed the might of CSR-Readymix in the court proceedings. CSR fielded a brace of expensive lawyers, consultants and advisers, led by John Whitehouse, then a director of Madden Dunhill Butler. On the first day of proceedings, Muir secured the admission to the proceedings of strong opposing submissions by the majority of Government agencies to the original development application, including a damning report by Sydney Water. But Muir, with no knowledge of Court proceedings except for a 15-minute briefing from a sympathetic barrister, was no match for the massed forces of CSR-Readymix, who had commissioned high profile barrister Peter McClellan QC.

Justice Paul Stein did reject the CSR-Readymix argument that key environmental concerns could be dealt with by an environmental management plan at a later date. Milo Dunphy, for the Colong Foundation, had successfully argued that the court must satisfy itself that reasonable environmental standards can be met at the time of a decision and that it cannot accept the promise of mitigating design measures as a solution to recognised management problems. But Stein's decision prompted a desperate flurry of effort by CSR-Readymix to develop an acceptable management plan for the proposal. On the last day of hearings the company presented a more sympathetic mine plan with better sediment controls and reduced scenic impact on the adjoining Nattai Wilderness area. The Colong Foundation's soil and water management experts could do little more than note the design improvements.

A misty morning on the Nattai River. This tranquil wild river was protected with the dedication of the Nattai National Park in 1991.

Ironstone bands are a common formation in sandstones of the Sydney Basin.

While the Court case failed to stop approval of the quarry, it did succeed in strengthening community support for a wilderness national park and gained considerable political attention. In April 1990, Tim Moore announced that Cabinet would soon consider the Nattai wilderness proposal. In May, Bob Carr, then Leader of the Opposition, threw out a challenge by stating that the Nattai would be part of a Labor Government's next round of parks. He had recently enjoyed a bushwalk with Alex Colley, Keith Muir and Henry Gold to Bonnum Pic, a narrow peninsula of the Wanganderry Tableland extending into the Burragorang Valley.

In September 1991, Milo Dunphy telephoned the former Education Minister, Dr Terry Metherell, who had recently become an independent member of Parliament after leaving the Liberal Party. Dr Metherell together with Independents Clover Moore, Dr Peter Macdonald and John Hatton then held the balance of power over the Greiner Government in the Lower House of Parliament. Milo Dunphy immediately suggested that the establishment of a new Nattai National Park should be the first issue on Metherell's agenda. This was agreed and a Nattai Park Bill was soon developed and was introduced into Parliament in October 1991.

Tim Moore then enthusiastically developed a scheme that would secure the reservation of all the remaining lands between the Nattai and the Blue Mountains National Park on the northern side of the Burragorang Valley. When debate resumed on 15 November, Moore presented a scheme for a 65,000 hectare Nattai National Park with a wilderness core of 29,824 hectares, together with four new State Recreation Areas totalling a further 30,000 hectares.

The Metherell/Moore park scheme did not proceed smoothly, though it did proceed quickly. The purpose of the State Recreation Areas was not recreation but a concession to the mining industry. The original 75,000 hectare Nattai proposal had affected a tiny portion of an 11,370 square kilometre exploration licence for coal seam methane gas owned by the petroleum giant Amoco. The company

The Nattai Wilderness forms the southern division of the Greater Blue Mountains World Heritage Area.

Cliffs near Cape Horn, Gardens of Stone National Park.

was outraged and the Premier, Mr Nick Greiner, claimed that overriding exploration licences would influence the State's triple-A credit rating. In response, the original proposal was reduced by exclusions for state recreation areas and a 60-metre depth restriction on the national park. However, on 13 December 1991, the Nattai Wilderness was gazetted without restrictions, becoming the first area to be declared under the *Wilderness Act*. The wilderness was secured. Interestingly, the Mt Flora hard rock quarry, approved in 1990, has not been developed.

Three months after the Nattai win, it was revealed that Dr Metherell had been negotiating for the position of Director General of the NSW Environment Protection Authority. Just before a political whirlpool around Metherell drew in Tim Moore, and closed around the Greiner Government, Milo Dunphy and Keith Muir negotiated into legislation a schedule for the public exhibition of wilderness assessments across the State, paving the way for wilderness conservation in NSW. So while everyone else in NSW was venting rancour on Messrs Metherell and Moore, the Colong Foundation quietly consolidated important wilderness conservation initiatives in the dying days of the Greiner administration.

□ □ □

The Gardens of Stone, 30 km north of Lithgow, embrace much of the Newnes Plateau and the broken stone country between the Plateau and the Airly-Genowlan Mesa to the north in the Capertee

View south up the Rocky Creek gorge toward Newnes Plateau and the southern extension of the Gardens of Stone National Park.

This quietly flowing stream can, after heavy rainfall, turn into a torrent raging through the canyon.

Valley. The area remains to this day the only part of Myles Dunphy's Greater Blue Mountains National Park proposal that is not fully protected.

The key features of the Gardens of Stone are the 'pagodas', which are typically rock pinnacles that contain resistant ironstone layers weathered out of the intervening sandstone matrix to produce spectacular geological features. The pagoda formations vary from the ironstone 'platy form' pagodas, unique to the area, to the smooth variety somewhat reminiscent of the Bungle Bungles of Western Australia.

In mid-1984, Rodney Falconer, a member of the Colo Committee, discovered a number of rock falls from cliffs, together with cracks and fissures. The damage was associated with the Angus Place Colliery on the western edge of the Newnes Plateau, above Lambs Creek near Wolgan Gap. Spurred on by this threat of further coal-related damage, Rodney Falconer and David Blackwell had, by September 1985, completed a submission to Premier Wran for a 'Gardens of Stone' 38,000 hectare addition to Wollemi National Park. This submission, on behalf of the Colo Committee, the Colong Foundation for Wilderness and the Federation of Bushwalking Clubs, was not the first proposal for reservation of the area. In 1966, the National Trust had proposed a 'Pinnacles State Park' and, in 1984, Stephen Lord on behalf of the National Parks Association produced a proposal for a south-western addition to Wollemi National Park.

Following the presentation of the park plan, a succession of NSW Parliamentarians visited the area all curious to see this spectacular pagoda landscape that they had heard so much about. The first, in December 1985, was Bob Carr, then Minister for the Environment and Planning, who visited the area with members of the Colong Committee, the Lower Blue Mountains Conservation Society, as well as John Whitehouse, then Director of the National Parks and Wildlife Service. The party was stunned by a series of recent cliff collapses that extended for hundreds of metres. A new technology had caused this damage, longwall mining, which removes coal in large panels without retention of coal pillars to prevent movement of the land surface.

The local *Lithgow Mercury* led opposition to the park. The paper had predicted the loss of 50 timber workers' jobs if the plan went ahead and forecast that a huge demonstration would meet the inspection party. But on the day there were no timber workers to be seen. A representative of the mining industry later maintained that no one really cared about cliff collapses on Newnes Plateau – after all, not many people visited the area. A few weeks later the *Katoomba Echo* predicted the loss of hundreds of mining jobs and raised the spectre of Lithgow becoming a ghost town. Contrary to this pre-emptive media strike, the objective of the Gardens of Stone proposal was not the closure of mines, only the restriction of mining so that it would not cause damage to cliffs, swamps and pagodas. The pine plantations on the Newnes Plateau were also excluded from the proposal. The remaining economic resources were very limited, but misinformed local opposition to the park proposal continued.

In May 1986, the Colong Foundation received a letter from Bob Carr saying that, because the area was already committed to coal mining or was actively mined, the impact of underground mining on surface environments was such that it would be unacceptable as a national park. Parts of the area had also been committed to the continued supply of Blue Mountains Ash for mining timber.

Rodney Falconer's representations to the Minister for Environment and Planning and the Minister for Natural Resources regarding the mining damage resulted in a landscape assessment. An initial assessment reported in 1985 that rockfalls, caused by mining subsidence, had 'significantly down-graded the visual quality of the landscape'. Following the inspection by Bob Carr, more encouraging news came from Mr Ken Gabb, Minister for Natural Resources, who wrote at the end of July 1986 that Newcom Collieries had agreed that future longwall mining panels would be reoriented to protect the Wolgan Valley escarpment, the upper reaches of Lambs Creek and Blackfellows Hand Cave. These

Cliffs and pagodas near McLeans Pass, Gardens of Stone National Park.

undertakings only moderated the damage, and a decade later it was discovered that 55 cliff falls had occurred as a result of mining operations at the Angus Place Colliery between 1985 and 1988.

Despite the damage, and the limitations described by Bob Carr, conservationists could see no reason why the cliff lines and the land not required for mining or timber should not be protected. To make the project more politically acceptable, it was apparently necessary for the coal-rich areas to be removed. Another ten-year campaign was then necessary before the northern part of the botanically diverse Newnes Plateau, a key element of the Gardens of Stone, could be protected.

A breakthrough came in April 1993, when the Blue Mountains City Council unanimously resolved to support a modified Gardens of Stone proposal by the Colong Foundation for Wilderness. The proposal involved two stages: while the 18,030 hectares outside existing mining leases would be reserved immediately, another 25,200 hectares of the original proposal within mining leases were proposed for further investigation to see if mining methods could be moderated to protect the main values of the area. The new proposal also sought immediate protection for the Airly-Genowlan mesa, which was then under application by Novacoal for a mining lease, and protection too for part of the Clarence Colliery exploration area that was within the Wollemi Wilderness. Development pressure was again increasing when an adverse report of the Commission of Inquiry into the Airly Colliery proposal was handed down in February 1994 recommending that the mine proceed, albeit with some protection zones for key pagoda features and for historic oil shale ruins.

In April, Robert Webster, the Minister for Planning, issued Novacoal a development consent which covered the Airly but not the Genowlan Mesa. The Colong Foundation was very concerned that the approval conditions would have no effect because recent amendments to the *Mining Act, 1992* prevented any consent conditions made under planning legislation from controlling mining activities.

View across a pagoda formation to the Gardens of Stone National Park. The sandstone mesa of Pantoneys Crown in the upper Capertee Valley is the park's focal point.

Ferns clothe the steep walls of this canyon.

The cliff falls that had occurred at Angus Place could therefore occur at an Airly mine despite the controls imposed by Webster. For this reason, the Colong Foundation pressed on with the national park proposal in an attempt to protect the outstanding 5,500 hectare Airly-Genowlan Mesa, even though the imposition of a mining lease over the area seemed inevitable.

Penny Figgis, Vice President of the Australian Conservation Foundation, and Keith Muir of the Colong Foundation, visited Lithgow Council in June in an attempt to mollify increasing local opposition to the park. A site inspection of the proposal was conducted in the presence of councillors and representatives of the United Mine Workers Union (UMWU), including Clr Howard Fisher and Mr Wayne McAndrew. The spectacular scenery of the proposal failed to impress the party who could only imagine the issue in terms of coal lost to industry. An inspection shortly after of the 11,000 volt electric-powered underground longwall mining machine at the Baal Bone Colliery confirmed for conservationists that modern mining machinery would continue to destroy the pagoda landscapes. In August, Lithgow Council rejected a proposal by its Environmental Services Manager to conditionally support the Gardens of Stone proposal because the park could be reserved without impact on coal mining. Clr Howard Fisher, President of the UMWU, moved a motion to reject the proposal, and at the end of the meeting Lithgow's only green councillor resigned in protest.

Meanwhile, Clover Moore, one of three Independents in the Lower House, had agreed to sponsor legislation to implement the Colong Foundation's Gardens of Stone park plan. The Gardens of Stone proposal initially stalled when Labor would not support Dr Peter Macdonald's National Parks and Wildlife (New Areas) Bill, which Clover Moore had planned to amend to create the new Gardens of Stone park. On 29 November 1994, in the run-up to the state election, and seeing a political advantage over Labor in supporting a green issue, the Fahey Coalition Government approved a Gardens of Stone National Park of 11,780 hectares. Most of the park additions adjoined the Wollemi National Park, with a western link protecting the Capertee Valley headwaters.

Labor opposed the new park, supporting instead Mr Mick Clough, who held the seat of Bathurst by a slim margin. The Shadow Environment Minister, Pam Allan, said that in this instance Labor was standing for jobs ahead of national parks. Of course this position was pure politics as there were no coal resources in the newly created park, and 3,000 pro-park signatures collected in Bathurst contradicted Mr Clough's claim that only city conservationists supported the park. However, the incoming Carr Government later consolidated the new park in December 1995 with the addition of 3,600 hectares excised from Newnes State Forest to protect Rocky Creek canyon. Mr Clough's opposition to the park was by that stage no longer relevant to the fate of government.

The most scenic part of the original proposal, the Airly-Genowlan Mesa, was omitted from the park. This area contains the most striking pagoda formations in Australia. It also contains significant historic relics of oil shale mining days of the 1880s. The Department of Mineral Resources, oblivious to the area's conservation value, issued Novacoal a mining lease in October 1993 covering Airly Mesa but not the even more spectacular Genowlan area to the east. The Airly lease was later taken over by Centennial Coal but as yet has not been developed. The mine remains a dubious proposition because available markets require coal transport by road to the coast, which is too expensive and opposed by the Roads and Traffic Authority.

After 10 years of campaigning and debate, a Gardens of Stone National Park was created. No jobs were lost nor coal output reduced. Centennial Coal remains unable to develop the Airly mine as it has not secured supply contracts from the nearby power stations. The *National Parks and Wildlife Amendment Act, 2001*, providing for State Conservation Areas, allows mining as well as protection of high conservation value areas and may assist with the protection of Airly. The key problem remains just how much conservation can be achieved when the coal is extracted, the land surface subsides, upland swamps dry up, scenic pagodas crack and cliffs fall.

View from the Gardens of Stone escarpment to Pantoneys Crown, the Airly-Genowlan Mesa on the horizon.

CHAPTER 7

The World Heritage Campaign

by Keith Muir

EARLY in 1984, by which time most of the Blue Mountains had been reserved in national parks, the Colong Committee decided to seek World Heritage Listing. The area had already been placed on the register of Australia's National Estate in 1976 after Colong had commissioned architect Michael Bell to define the area and assess its threats. World Heritage Listing would be the ultimate preservation measure, invoking the responsibility of the Federal Government and the World Heritage Centre of UNESCO. Initial applications for grants to pursue the proposal were, however, rejected by both State and Federal agencies.

The Colong Committee, renamed the Colong Foundation in 1986, decided to explore the possibility of voluntary funding. It was decided that, if the submission was published as a book, some if not all of the cost might be recovered. A Heritage Book Fund was set up, to which the Colong Foundation contributed $2,100, with donations of a further $4,000 promised. Professional voluntary assistance, including typesetting, visuals, publicity and distribution, was obtained from a number of sources. The artist Graham Cox, whose paintings of the Blue Mountains were much in demand, offered to make available a reproduction of one of his paintings along with a substantial donation. Pat Thompson, who had suggested Colong might publish the proposal as a book, would distribute the book through his company Envirobook. Henry Gold would provide a selection of photographic images of the beautiful and remote areas beyond the tourist centres. Roger Rigby, General Manager of Clemenger Proximity Agency, would attend to the layout of two publicity posters, and Jenni Gormley offered to design and typeset the book. Dr Geoff Mosley, whom the Foundation had approached to write a submission and who had expressed his concern that the Blue Mountains 'were getting further and further back in the queue', was keen to get on with the job.

Dr Mosley was eminently qualified to write the book. From 1981 to 1988 he was a member of the IUCN's Commission on National Parks and Protected Areas and he had refereed seven Australian World Heritage nominations. The book, *Blue Mountains for World Heritage*, was launched by Bob Carr, then Leader of the Opposition, on 6 December 1989. He described it as 'a milestone in conservation'. Environment Minister, Tim Moore, and the Member for Blue Mountains, Barry Morris, also supported the project.

To qualify for listing, natural properties needed to satisfy one of four criteria. Dr Mosley credited the Mountains as qualifying under three of these criteria. The first is that the site must 'be an outstanding example representing a major stage of the earth's evolutionary history'. He described the Mountains as:

> The most outstanding example in the world of the uplift and erosion of a sedimentary upheaval of the Permo-Triassic period. The depression of successive sedimentary layers of varying compression in a major trough (the Sydney Basin) between two highlands was followed by its uplift as one of the consequences of the rifting and sea floor spreading in the Tasman Sea area, and possibly also as a result of regional isostatic rebound. The lowland area on the seaward side of the mountains appears to have been created by similar forces dragging down the land to the east of the Lapstone Monocline…

> The Blue Mountains contains one of the richest assemblages of xeromorphic (adapted to drought and poor soils) plants in Australia and therefore the world… The dominance of the forest flora by many

Early morning, the Grose Valley, Blue Mountains National Park.

species of the virtually endemic *Eucalyptus* genera is a result of the long period of relative isolation of the Australian plate after the breakup from Gondwana and before it came close to the lands of the northern plates. This development is reflected in the present day pattern of vegetation distribution in which the rainforest still remains on the richer soils but the vegetation on the generally poor soils is sclerophyll open forest. The vegetation therefore represents a major event in the earth's history – the breakup of Gondwana and the development of the distinctive vegetation cover adapted to the peculiar conditions of the Australian environment.

The second qualifying point is that the site 'be an outstanding example representing significant ongoing geological processes, biological evolution and man's interaction with his natural environment…in the development of communities of plants and animals, landforms and marine areas and freshwater bodies'. Regarding significant ongoing geological processes, Dr Mosley wrote:

> The processes of weathering which are slowly dissecting the Blue Mountains plateau are of course ongoing. The debate about the process, which was begun by Darwin, Dana, Taylor and Craft, is being continued by Young and others today. Studies in the landforms of the Permo-Triassic area of the Sydney

Old growth Manna Gum (Eucalyptus viminalis) *forest on Mount Kerry in the northern Blue Mountains.*

Basin have already suggested that the revised denudation chronology may be needed for the tempo of geographic change around the world and the area is expected to yield further information on the subject.

And, analysing the Mountain's plant communities:

The vegetation is a classic representation of the xeromorphic assemblages which developed as a result of Australia's isolation and changing environment following the separation from Gondwana [and] although dominated by sclerophyll open forest, is extremely diverse. The site has over 1,200 species of vascular plants… This is the result of the high level of species diversity in the eucalypts and other xeromorphic plants… Because of its natural condition the vegetation is in a dynamic state of evolution… offer[ing] considerable scope for efforts to improve an understanding of eucalypt speciation. Also remarkable is the exceptional number of species with primitive characteristics.

The third qualifying point is that the site must 'contain superlative natural phenomena, formations or features, for instance, outstanding examples of the most important ecosystems, areas of exceptional natural beauty or exceptional combinations and cultural elements'. On this point Dr Mosley wrote:

Tens of millions of years of erosion have resulted in the Blue Mountains rivers becoming deeply entrenched in the sandstone plateau. The profound depths and massive bordering cliffs are the main natural wonders of the Blue Mountains. Many of these features occur in areas which are still remote wilderness. In fact, although Australia's largest population concentration is situated less than 100 kilometres to the east, the region… has the best wilderness of the open sclerophyll type in the world… The Wollemi Wilderness in particular, potentially over 400,000 hectares, is outstanding on a world scale. More compact, the Kanangra Wilderness, could eventually cover some 200,000 hectares.

Dr Mosley did not claim that the Blue Mountains qualified on the fourth criterion, that the Mountains 'contain the most important and significant habitats, where threatened species of animals or plants of outstanding universal value from the point of conservation or science still survive'. Although he did not claim that the area qualified on this point, he wrote that there were 157 plants and animals in the parks recognised as rare, endangered or restricted. Had the Wollemi Pine been discovered before he wrote the book, he might have claimed that the area qualified on this point too. Nor did he claim that the Mountains qualified as a cultural property, though he wrote that 'the claim with the best chance of success is the association of the Blue Mountains with conservation innovations, particularly the wilderness concept, which had a great and lasting influence on conservation development generally'.

Dr Mosley had made an authoritative and complete case for World Heritage listing, and it was supported by both the State and Federal Governments. The only opposition came from Dr Jim Thorsell, the IUCN's Chief World Heritage Adviser for Natural Areas, who in 1989 rated the chance of listing at less than 20 per cent. Despite Dr Mosley's compelling submission, it was only after a series of reports, assessments and reassessments of assessments, extending over nine years, that a nomination was presented to UNESCO. The Federal Government deferred consideration of the proposal in order to concentrate on nomination of Shark Bay and the sub-Antarctic islands although these, unlike the Blue Mountains, were remote from population centres.

Local conservation groups and the Colong Foundation formed a Blue Mountains World Heritage Group at a meeting held at Springwood on 16 August 1991. Addressing the meeting were Dr Mosley and several prominent members of the NSW Labor Party including Pam Allan, Shadow Minister for the Environment, Fay Lo Po, Member for Penrith, Bob Debus, candidate for the seat of Blue Mountains, and a number of candidates for the Blue Mountains City Council. Urging pressure on the State and Federal Governments, Pam Allan read a letter from the Prime Minister, Bob Hawke, who agreed with Bob Carr that the Blue Mountains was of considerable conservation and cultural significance. Support from the German Greens Party was tabled. The meeting resolved: to call on the Federal Government to start immediately on the process of nomination for 'inscription' on the World Heritage list; to call on the State Government and local councils to support the nomination; to form a committee of citizens to support the nomination; to see that the decisions of the meeting were carried out; to lobby the Government and community organisations; and to advocate and inform citizens about the World Heritage proposal.

On 26 March 1992, Dr Terry Metherell asked in the NSW Parliament what steps the Government was prepared to take to expedite the World Heritage nomination. The Premier, Nick Greiner, replied that there were two problems – the inadequate Blue Mountains sewerage system and the refusal of the Federal Government to share the costs of the very extensive studies that needed to be done. Fortunately, the sewerage problem was being addressed – Tim Moore had imposed an environmental levy which would help finance a $70 million sewerage scheme.

The Colong Foundation questioned why, in view of Dr Mosley's expert submission, further detailed studies were necessary. Dr Mosley quoted submissions for several other nominations that had been financed by the Federal Government. In August 1992, the Labor Opposition in the NSW Parliament expressed its total agreement with the Colong Foundation's endeavours on World Heritage and in December 1992, the Blue Mountains City Council appointed a World Heritage Listing Sub-Committee, chaired by the Mayor, and organised a forum of the 12 local councils involved in the World Heritage proposal. The forum was held on 19 March 1993. In addition to the councils, it was attended by state and federal parliamentarians, the National Parks and Wildlife Service, the Nature Conservation Council of NSW, the local community's Blue Mountains for World Heritage Committee and Dr Mosley. A program to achieve nomination by October 1994 was submitted by Mr Max Fragar on behalf of the Blue Mountains City Council… It proved, alas, a very premature program.

Early in 1994, the State and Federal Governments, after nearly four years of haggling over the cost, agreed to fund a $30,000 'preliminary study' of the World Heritage proposal. Dr Mosley tendered an application, but it was not acknowledged. The National Herbarium (based at the Royal Botanic Gardens, Sydney) completed the study in October 1994. In September 1994, the Wollemi Pine was discovered in a canyon in the northern Blue Mountains. It was thought to have become extinct 65 million years before and should have stimulated the World Heritage proposal. The National Herbarium stated in their study that the relictual rainforest flora of the Blue Mountains included some of the most primitive flowering plants in the world. However, release of the study was delayed because, according to the Minister for the Environment, the Hon. Chris Hartcher, further assessment was being done. Why further assessment of the 493 page National Herbarium study was necessary was not explained.

It was now five years since Dr Mosley's submission had been published. The NSW Government, now led by Liberal Premier John Fahey, had procrastinated. The reasons for this were not revealed, but it was probably due to the anti-conservation elements in their ranks, as evidenced by their opposition to wilderness declarations. The Government's slender majority Fahey felt, should not be risked.

The National Herbarium study was essentially an expanded and more detailed version of Dr Mosley's 135 page book, increasing the amount of supporting data and recommending considerable extensions to the area originally proposed. It described the Blue Mountains and surrounding plateaus as an 'outstanding natural property of World Heritage status with universal values for science, conservation and natural beauty'. In support of this, the study listed a number of outstanding features. The eucalypt forests and woodlands were some of the most unusual in the world. The wilderness areas were of world conservation significance as a centre of, and habitat for, a diverse range of rare, threatened and endemic plants. The remoteness and primitiveness of the wilderness areas made them some of the most

Clockwise from top left: Grevillea *(Grevillea acanthifolia)*, *unique to the Blue Mountains;* Flannel Flower *(Actinotus helianthi);*
Honey Flower, *also known as* Mountain Devil *(Lambertia formosa);* Tea Tree *(Leptospermum macrocarpum) also unique to the Blue Mountains.*

important places on earth. The most distinctive features of these areas were their long and significant record of landform evolution. The unique combination of geography, dissected plateau surfaces, low nutrient soils and significant biodiversity values set the Blue Mountains and surrounding plateaus apart from any other World Heritage area. These qualities were all covered in Dr Mosley's book. The Herbarium study had only added one point to those his book had covered – that the main recreational threats within the national parks were associated with four-wheel driving and horseriding.

In March 1995, a Labor Government was elected in NSW, and by late 1995 the new Environment Minister, Pam Allan, advised that the World Heritage Properties Ministerial Committee had established a Steering Committee of NSW and Federal officials to oversee the preparation of a nomination for the Blue Mountains. In February 1996, Senator John Faulkner, the Federal Labor Environment Minister, had announced another assessment of the assessments. An expert panel, comprising Professor Jamie Kirkpatrick, a botanical expert from the University of Tasmania, Ms Sharon Sullivan, Executive Director of the Australian Heritage Commission and an expert in pre-history, and Professor Cliff Ollier an expert in geomorphology from the University of New England, was appointed to provide advice on World Heritage listing. Senator Faulkner said that the nomination could be submitted by 30 June 1996 if these experts confirmed the existence of World Heritage values.

Mount Yengo, an ancient volcanic peak, rises above the surrounding sandstone plateau.

A slot canyon. Canyons like this have been carved over eons of time by water action from creeks finding a way through joints and other weaknesses in the sandstone.

The nomination did not meet the submission deadline. Premier Bob Carr said on 29 August that the NSW bid to have the Blue Mountains declared World Heritage was jeopardised by the lack of cooperation from the newly elected federal Howard Government.

The experts had submitted three separate opinions, resulting in uncertainty and indecision. Professor Ollier did not consider that the Blue Mountains represented the best example of any geomorphological theme and as such the area would be unlikely to satisfy the World Heritage criteria. Ms Sullivan reported that there was a basis for a cultural submission based on Aboriginal art in the area. Professor Kirkpatrick identified the eucalypts as being sufficient to satisfy the World Heritage criteria. It was unlikely that listing would be approved on a submission based on Aboriginal art and doubtful that it would be approved on the sole basis of a eucalypt theme. Professor Ollier's advice elicited further supporting data from Australia's best qualified World Heritage authority and from a leading geologist. Dr Mosley wrote:

> Professor Ollier claims (1) that the features of the dissected sandstone plateaus 'are better represented elsewhere in the world' and (2) that 'as sandstones are the second most common geology on the globe, examples based on it would have to be extremely spectacular to be considered as being of world heritage value'. These are worthless comments, because with regard to (1) he says nothing about where such features are better represented. There does not appear to be any dissected sandstone plateau of this type on the world heritage list at present and I am not aware of any better example in existence. With regard to (2), the fact that sandstone is a common rock does not mean that there are necessarily any more representative or better samples elsewhere. What is significant is that an important part of the earth's surface is unrepresented on the list at present. Until Professor Ollier, or anyone else, is able to provide factual comparative information with which to dispute the claim that the Blue Mountains plateaus have outstanding universal values in terms of this criterion, this justification, as documented, should be used for the nomination… Professor Ollier criticises the work of the Royal Botanic Gardens for not addressing international comparisons when he himself fails to do this.

Professor Brian Marshall an expert geomorphologist from the University of Technology, Sydney also criticised Professor Ollier's view that the features of the sandstone plateaus were better represented elsewhere. Although Professor Ollier was correct in stating that this type of tectonic boundary is common at a global scale, the statement had negligible significance, since the pre-existing rock types and structure, and the local climatic effects, can induce different geological and geomorphological expressions. Any implication that the Blue Mountains had strict geological and geomorphological parallels in other continents, or in Australia, was poorly founded. Professor Marshall considered that the Blue Mountains was an outstanding example of the geology and climate-specific geomorphology that characterise certain passive continental margins. Disregarding specific climate differences, examples in other continents may have a higher escarpment, steeper gorge, or mightier waterfall, but the Blue Mountains provided an outstanding set of well described, accurately dated and accessible landforms that clearly satisfied the first two of the World Heritage criteria.

In his review of the National Herbarium Report, CSIRO Chief Research Scientist, Dr Bryan Barlow, praised the work of the consultants, saying their report 'could become a most compelling proposal for World Heritage listing. All the necessary information has been assembled and there is no good reason why the nomination should not go to the Commonwealth Government in the near future'.

On 18 December 1997, Democrat Leader Meg Lees, Democrat Senator Lyn Allison and Liberal Senator Tierney of the Senate Reference Committee inquiring into the Federal Government's Environmental Powers, visited the Blue Mountains. They were accompanied by representatives of the Colong Foundation, the Blue Mountains Conservation Society and a retinue that included a Senate

With increasing distance, the green hue of the eucalypt forest shifts towards blue, which gives the Mountains their name.

Reference Committee Secretary and Research Officer, and a Hansard reporter. The purpose of the Committee's inspection was to ascertain whether the Federal Government's nomination process was consistent with its obligations under the World Heritage Convention. The party examined controversial development sites, scenic vantage points, the urban sprawl along Kings Tableland and sewerage works under way to divert sewage out of the proposed World Heritage area. They also viewed John Weileys' movie, *The Edge,* showing the natural heritage of the Blue Mountains.

Early in 1998, the State and Federal Governments provided $80,000 for a nomination for World Heritage listing. It was announced at the inaugural meeting of the community-based reference group set up to oversee the preparation of the nomination that both the Federal and State Governments were committed to a eucalypt-based nomination. This decision was strongly criticised by the reference group because such a thematically based nomination was outside the specifications of the World Heritage assessment criteria. There was also a real risk that the World Heritage Committee would refer the nomination back to the Federal Government for further work, as had happened with the Macquarie Island proposal which was based on a geological theme. In a submission to the Senate Reference Committee, the Colong Foundation pointed out that the eucalypt theme was irresponsibly dismissive of geomorphological values.

On 18 February 1998, to avoid further delay arising from a Federal proposal for yet another review, Environment Minister Pam Allan announced that the nomination would be completed by the following June. It was hoped it would be approved before the Sydney Olympic Games in 2000. The nomination was supervised by Joan Domicelj, who had only six weeks to complete it for dispatch to the World Heritage Centre of UNESCO before 30 June, in time for consideration during 1998. The exponential proliferation of assessments was now over, but it remained to convince the World Heritage Committee.

❑ ❑ ❑

Keith Muir, Director, and Tom Widdup, Assistant Director, of the Colong Foundation attended the World Heritage Conference in Cairns in November 2000. This was to be the conference which would determine the fate of the Blue Mountains Heritage nomination. They found themselves immersed in a political game of bewildering complexity.

Australia, as host nation to the Cairns Conference, and in possession of the chair of the World Heritage Committee, could not speak to its Blue Mountains nomination. Two World Heritage Bureau meetings and the 1999 World Heritage Committee meeting had recommended deferral of the nomination, largely at the insistence of Dr Jim Thorsell, the chief World Heritage advisor for natural areas. Dr Thorsell would sum up the case against the nomination and then, if Australia was lucky, the Committee would consider the nomination.

Not only was Dr Thorsell opposed to the Blue Mountains nomination but he also considered that there were too many World Heritage sites. He said that sites, including two in Australia, were being listed against the recommendations of the IUCN and there was too much lobbying and politics in the World Heritage listing process. The Colong Foundation had to overcome this opposition to the nomination without damaging Dr Thorsell's standing as a respected conservationist and World Heritage expert.

The Howard Government's position on World Heritage created several major political problems that threatened to dash the listing chances for the Blue Mountains. These problems were related to:
- the proposed Jabiluka uranium mine within World Heritage-listed Kakadu National Park;
- the Government's resistance to the Mirrar Aboriginal people's cultural concerns with the proposed Jabiluka mine;
- a controversial proposal by the Government to prevent World Heritage sites being considered for 'In Danger' listing without the approval of the relevant national government; and

Waratah (Telopea speciosissima), *state floral emblem of New South Wales.*

- another Government proposal to downgrade the status of the World Heritage Committee's scientific, cultural and environmental advisory bodies (ICOMOS and IUCN) and restrict monitoring and scrutiny of the care of World Heritage sites to government agencies (non-government organisations would not have a role).

The Federal Environment Minister, Senator Hill, said that his Government was opposed to international scrutiny of Australia's World Heritage site management and that the World Heritage Committee was not set up as a watchdog. The Australian Government wanted to eviscerate what Dr Thorsell called the 'bible' (the operational guidelines to the World Heritage Convention), apparently to justify mining uranium in the World Heritage listed Kakadu National Park, and avoid further scrutiny. This proposal threatened the 'integrity' of world heritage sites and Dr Thorsell and many non-government organisations were understandably concerned.

The NSW State Government delegation to the Cairns Conference proved absolutely crucial. It ensured that support for Blue Mountains nomination was distinguished from the controversial positions of the Australian Government. There is also no doubt that Environment Australia, the Australian Government's national conservation agency, by having a broad range of people and talents available at the Conference, was able to utilise all strategic opportunities as they arose.

Unlike the Australian Government's objectives, the Colong Foundation and the NSW delegation had but one objective: to convert the Conference delegates into Blue Mountains supporters. Unless this was achieved, Dr Thorsell's position, twice confirmed by the World Heritage Bureau, would carry the day.

The Foundation assembled posters, a French translation of its main case, and illustrated lobby books to assist the advocacy of its three representatives (John Sinclair, Tom Widdup and Keith Muir). Its lobby book consisted of quotes from supporting experts and outstanding photographs by Henry Gold. Over 40 books were circulated amongst delegates, many of whom considered them to be collectors' items.

The support of 12 internationally respected plant scientists, including Professor Sir Robert May, President-elect of the Royal Society, was the cornerstone of the Foundation's argument. Surely, if the IUCN had accepted expert advice regarding the World Heritage values of eucalypt forests, then it was reasonable to expect acceptance of the same experts' advice on the Blue Mountains. It was also obvious to UNESCO and the IUCN that the Colong Foundation and the Australian Government were going to continue to pursue the nomination. The media were following the story very closely.

On Sunday 26 November, the day before the Conference, at a World Heritage Management Symposium held at James Cook University, the Colong Foundation explained that they had already used the World Heritage Convention to advantage because, since the Foundation's Blue Mountains World Heritage proposal, two new national parks and three new wilderness areas had been created within the nomination area. As well, the raising of Warragamba Dam wall, which would have flooded river valleys in the Kanangra-Boyd National Park, had been rejected, and a 65 kilometre sewerage tunnel, costing hundreds of millions of dollars, had been constructed to stop sewage pollution. Even the proposed Badgerys Creek Airport, which entailed flights over the Mountains, and a proposed super-highway in the Blue Mountains National Park, were presented as recent examples where the World Heritage Convention had lent a hand to protect the area. This news appeared to impress the IUCN.

The World Heritage Committee is composed of 21 voting nations, but many other signatory countries attended the Conference as observers. A vital task for the Foundation was to meet the delegates from all voting countries and explain to them the worth of the Blue Mountains nomination. Many Conference delegates had already been informed by Environment Australia. The NSW National Parks and Wildlife Service had taken representatives from Mexico and Hungary, as well as Mr Mounir Bouchenaki, Assistant Director General of UNESCO, over the area by helicopter.

Heath and the rare Blue Mountains Mallee Ash (Eucalyptus stricta).

On Monday 27 November, it was obvious that there were certain countries that would be very supportive, others that were open to new information, and a small number that, for various reasons, would be very hard to convince. South Africa, China and Canada (Dr Thorsell's home country) initially appeared less interested in the Foundation's approaches.

By Monday afternoon it turned out that Senator Hill would not have to battle for the Jabiluka uranium mine, since the World Heritage Committee's scientific panel had apparently accepted the Government's contention that the mine posed no risk to the World Heritage values in the adjacent national park. The issue of protecting cultural values in Kakadu National Park remained unresolved and was put off until the following year. The World Heritage Committee's position on Kakadu, whilst unfortunately favourable to the proposed Jabiluka mine, was ironically an advantage to the Blue Mountains, as conflict on the floor of the Conference was avoided.

The Australian Government's voluntary deferral of its proposals to weaken the operational guidelines to the World Heritage Convention pushed that issue aside. Australia instead allowed subsequent legal advice to inform the World Heritage Committee on whether it could decide to place properties on the World Heritage 'In Danger' list independent of the concerns of the affected government. Given these outcomes, Senator Hill's ongoing diplomatic efforts on Tuesday and Wednesday, including dining with key delegations, were focussed on the Blue Mountains nomination.

Behind the scenes, the all important technical work on the Blue Mountains nomination was achieved by representatives of Environment Australia. They negotiated an acceptable solution for the IUCN to overcome Dr Thorsell's opposition, but these negotiations would have been hopeless if the

Mist rising from Pitts Amphitheatre swirls over Narrow Neck Peninsula.

The Grose Wilderness at dawn.

Australian and NSW support teams had not won the sympathy of most of the delegates during the first day of the Conference.

Professor Adrian Phillips, the Chairperson of the World Commission of Protected Areas, agreed to speak to the Conference on the Blue Mountains after Dr Thorsell. He would note that the nomination was a 'finely-balanced case' and that Australia had moved to create a national list of potential World Heritage areas. Professor Phillips, on his own initiative, mentioned the south-west of Western Australia and the Australian Alps as two eucalypt forest areas that should be considered for World Heritage listing.

On presenting the Blue Mountains nomination to the conference, Dr Thorsell criticised the nomination but acknowledged that some of the integrity issues, such as the proposed Badgerys Creek airport, had been addressed. Professor Phillips ably supported the nomination and opened the way for the 21 voting members of the World Heritage Committee to consider its fate.

Thailand, Malta, Korea, Morocco, Hungary and Mexico spoke in favour before the 21 voting nations made their decision. The delegates from Canada and South Africa were initially unsure, but were convinced by the body of scientific support. Three nations highlighted the Wollemi Pine. Thailand, who led the debate for listing, ensured that the biodiversity of the area was recognised, as well as its eucalypt forests. In an amusing speech, the Thailand delegate argued that if the habitat of the Komodo Dragon can be listed, why not the habitat of the Platypus? Thailand questioned Dr Thorsell's assessment and supported the nomination on criteria 2 and 4. The IUCN had indicated that it could accept an inscription on criterion 2 only. In the end, none of the delegates opposed the listing on the grounds of criteria 2 and 4, although Finland asked how many types of eucalypt were in the nomination area and how many were needed to qualify the area for listing.

The Greater Blue Mountains area was inscribed on the World Heritage list at 6.30 pm EST on 29 November 2000, for its diversity of eucalypt forests (criterion 2) and as a living laboratory of natural biodiversity, including its ancient plants as exemplified by the Wollemi Pine (criterion 4). In the flurry that surrounded the decision, its superlative scenery was unfortunately overlooked.

A pavement of tessellated sandstone above a cliff edge in the Grose Wilderness.

CHAPTER 8

Threats to the World Heritage Area

The Colong, Boyd, Colo, Nattai and Gardens of Stone campaigns prevented many major threats to the natural environment of the Blue Mountains. Any of these could would have been disastrous to the campaign for World Heritage listing had they not been stopped. Today other threats continue to endanger the integrity of the area.

Resort Development

A continuing threat to the wilderness quality of the mountains has been the construction of tourist resorts on or above cliff edges. Such resorts enable guests to enjoy wilderness views in comfort, but for park visitors looking in the opposite direction they are an invasion of the natural environment. The first such resort was the 'Hydro Majestic' at Medlow Bath, constructed in 1904. In 1960, the developer Oswald Ziegler proposed an inappropriate, multi-million dollar resort on public land at Govetts Leap. In the words of Peter Meredith, in his book *Myles and Milo*:

> …the project 'involved the creation of a 3 million pound tourist village complex (perhaps $100 million in today's money) to be named 'Pioneer Village' on the cliff edge at Govetts Leap, overlooking the Grose Gorge and Blue Gum forest in the Blue Mountains. The complex would include: a hotel, with swimming pool, skating ring and squash courts; a village reminiscent of 1840s Sydney; a lift to the floor of the Govett Gorge immediately below the hotel; a music shell and amphitheatre; the faces of explorers carved into the cliffs; a fauna sanctuary that would house native Australian creatures; car parks; a golf course; a miniature railway; a heliport; a residential village; and a Cobb and Co. coach that would be ambushed by 'bushrangers' as it conveyed tourists along a scenic track. A later inclusion was a 'prehistoric land' that would have large models of extinct creatures, none known to have inhabited Australia.

The project was referred by Professor Ashworth of the Faculty of Architecture at the University of Sydney to the fledgling Loder and Dunphy architectural partnership. The partnership desperately needed the money and did not immediately turn down the job though the project was directly opposed to their conservation ideals. Instead, they suggested considerable modifications. The Minister for Lands and the Blue Mountains City Council supported a much greater scheme, including a hotel with accommodation for 600 and a 75 metre high observation tower. By the end of the year, Milo Dunphy had completely rejected any support for the proposal, saying that 'the process of ecological and scenic decay' it would initiate 'would mean the end of the natural beauty of the mountain valley'. He later claimed that 'we saved the site just by the delay we caused'. In view of the abandonment of the Govetts Leap resort project it was very appropriate that the site was the venue of the World Heritage celebration and dedication ceremony, held on 12 May 2001, even if most of the participants in the function were unaware of the resort proposal.

In 1983, the Fairmont Resort, a $25 million convention centre was proposed to be located on the 6th and 7th holes of Leura Golf Course, a hill site near the cliff edge overlooking the Kedumba Valley. The Blue Mountains City Council had rezoned the site for development. The Department of Environment and Planning could have required a detailed local environmental study, but merely requested the Council to prepare an environmental report. The report was completed by Nexus Environmental Studies Pty Ltd in three weeks. Nexus stated that 'in this very short time it has not been possible to explore all the issues which concern the community'. Council accepted the report before the detailed advice of the Department was available. All the Blue Mountains conservation bodies

Victoria Falls in the Grose Valley.

opposed the proposal. In its submission to a Commission of Inquiry the Colong Foundation stated that 'there is no way of concealing, screening, or otherwise disguising the environmental impact of a six to seven storey building, 20 metres high and 300 metres long, a parking area for 798 cars, a retirement village for 87 people, 18 holiday cabins and sundry other buildings, together with access, dams, etc. positioned on a headland'.

The development gained the approval of the Wran Government in 1985. The Opposition spokesman on the environment, Tim Moore MP, was 'appalled by the Government's decision… It is bad enough that the rights of local residents and environmentalists are being ignored, but the very process of law is being threatened by the legislation'. Following the passage of special legislation by the NSW Government to overcome a series of court challenges against the development by local conservationists, construction started at the end of 1985 and was finished in mid 1987.

Probably encouraged by Fairmont's success, two more proposals were made for resorts overlooking Blue Mountains wilderness. One of these was the proposal by the World Plan Executive Council for a 415 bed educational and recreational facility for transcendental meditation on the edge of Radiata Plateau, overlooking Mcgalong Creek. Like the Fairmont Resort, the proposal violated the specific objectives of the Blue Mountains Environmental Management Plan adopted in 1985 to protect the Blue Mountains' unique landscape. The most relevant of these objectives were: to conserve natural ecological elements; to maintain and enhance the natural bushland buffer between towns; to ensure that new developments are located and managed so as to reduce the threat from bushfires (the site was on the top of a ridge); and to discourage development on the urban fringe. The proposal was strongly opposed by Pam Allan in the Legislative Assembly, by the Blue Mountains Conservation Society and other conservation organisations, and by local residents. This time the opposition was successful.

The other proposal was Earth Sanctuaries' plan for a $20 million resort on the Canyon Colliery lease at the source of the Grose River. Like the Oswald Zeigler 1960 proposal for a resort at Govetts Leap, this 1998 proposal would have overlooked the Grose Wilderness. The lease was previously part of the Blue Mountains National Park and conservationists strongly advocated its return to the park now that the mining was completed. They did not oppose the siting of the resort outside parklands. The Member for Blue Mountains, Bob Debus, accepted the conservationists' case and the majority of the colliery lease was returned to the Blue Mountains National Park in March 1999.

Urban Sprawl

Urban expansion in the Blue Mountains has created many environmental problems which successive planning schemes have sought to redress. The 1991 local environmental plan, produced by Blue Mountains City Council, emphasised the importance of preserving the natural features of the mountains from development. Accordingly, Mr Mike Eades, a Council officer engaged to work on the plan, identified: erosion-prone areas, sensitive vegetation regions such as rainforests, heathlands and alluvial forests, hanging swamps which feed the waterfalls, environmentally sensitive escarpment lines, the large natural areas between towns, bushfire hazard areas, and water catchment areas which feed creeks and waterfalls. The plan, however, facilitated low density urban sprawl along narrow ridgelines (using euphemistically titled Residential Bushland Conservation and Residential Bushland development zones), this sprawl being the main factor degrading the Mountains landscape.

The plan failed to prevent environmentally degrading projects such as development at Echo Point, the rezoning of Bodington Hill and a subdivision of a Linden Creek tributary which breached 20 principles of the plan. An amendment to the plan, passed in March 2001, gave better protection to the most environmentally sensitive urban fringe areas that were very vulnerable to fire and not connected to sewerage. Environmental abuses within existing towns, such as damage to stream-side vegetation, were not curtailed. The new law recognised the fringe area problems of steeply sloping land, and it limited land clearing and subdivision. The plan did not rule out development in such areas if, in the opinion of Council, certain conditions were met. Even its definition of 'development-excluded land', which embraced environmentally sensitive vegetation, rare flora, stream banks, slopes exceeding 20 degrees, rock outcrops and escarpment, permitted development if Council is satisfied the proposal 'has no adverse environmental impact'. The Colong Foundation has called for a consistent local environmental plan that would protect the World Heritage Area with effective development controls.

The Blue Mountains urban environment is one of the most vulnerable in the state, being prone to some of the highest fire risks in Australia. Mountain topography, and the bushlands which surround and intrude into it, make it subject to disastrous bushfires which have destroyed up to 150 houses at a time. This has led to calls for frequent broad-area burning away from the urban perimeter. But this is not appropriate, because eucalypt woodlands, while fire-adapted, contain many species that do not cope with regular firing. Frequent firing reduces plant diversity, which is the key World Heritage value, and removes ground cover that binds the sandy Blue Mountains soil. Massive sheet erosion occurs when heavy rain after a fire strips away the thin soils, causing permanent environmental damage. Fires also wipe out fauna populations and destroy old growth vegetation. Often it is the oldest plants that provide most of the nesting and roosting places for native animals. Fuel-reduction burns should be performed close to built up areas where they are most effective in protecting homes. Planning laws designed to restrict residential development in bushfire-prone areas now limit risk, but Blue Mountains residents need to regularly protect themselves by removing combustible materials from around their homes.

Some progress has been accomplished in pollution control. Before the construction of the $250 million sewerage tunnel from Katoomba to Winmalee, all the mountain streams flowing from urban areas, including those draining into the Warragamba Dam (Sydney's main water supply), were badly polluted due to inadequate local treatment. The scheme, hopefully with an extension

In 1973, 600,000 cubic metres of sandstone toppled into the Burragorang Valley, the result of underground coal mining. The surrounding area has since been reserved in the Burragorang State Conservation Area.

connecting Mount Victoria, Blackheath and Medlow Bath to the sewerage tunnel by a pipeline link, will enable all sewage from the Blue Mountains towns to be diverted out of the World Heritage Area. The Mittagong sewage treatment plant has been upgraded. Hilltop has been connected to it so that the Nattai River is now less polluted. Pollution of Blue Mountains streams is now mainly confined to rural and urban stormwater run-off and to the discharges from outlying properties which rely on septic tanks, the effluent from which is inadequately absorbed in the shallow sandy soils. A further threat arising from poor waste management is the trial application of sewage sludge on adjoining state forest areas to promote tree growth in the pine plantations on the Newnes Plateau. The sludge, like any concentrated fertiliser applied to the sandy soils of the area, is mobilised by rain and has the potential to badly pollute the pristine watercourses downstream within the World Heritage Area.

Nuisance Air Traffic

The proposed Badgerys Creek Airport site was within 5 km of the Blue Mountains National Park. Planned flight paths would have radiated to all points of the compass, crossing not only the Blue Mountains parks and townships but the western and southern suburbs of Sydney. Inevitably the protests of residents in these suburbs would have resulted in the diversion of flight paths over the Blue Mountains, which aircraft would cross not far above ground level, generating noise pollution across the

Jet fighter adventure flights shatter the solitude of the Wanganderry Tableland in the Nattai Wilderness, performing combat manoeuvres along the escarpment.

Under certain atmospheric conditions the valleys fill with mist, giving the appearance of a forbidding seashore.

wilderness. For this reason, the Colong Foundation played an active role in the Alliance for Airport Location Outside Sydney (Colong Director Keith Muir was its executive officer). It advocated the location of the 'second airport' in the Southern Highlands where it could be served by a proposed very fast train linking Canberra and Sydney. There are three topographically suitable locations on the highlands. The Colong Foundation favoured the Gundary Plains south of Goulburn, three-quarters of an hour by very fast train from Sydney and half-an-hour from Canberra.

Access to Badgerys Creek, as with Kingsford Smith Airport, would have been mainly by car from residential areas to the east and north, necessitating major road construction if traffic congestion through already overcrowded roads of western Sydney was to be mitigated. In January 1998, the NSW Government called on the Federal Government to immediately drop Badgerys Creek as an airport option. Pam Allan, then Minister for the Environment, said that pollution levels would rival those seen in Los Angeles and Mexico. Under such traffic conditions, the journey to Goulburn by very fast train would take little longer than a road journey to Badgerys Creek. Year after year the Badgerys Creek proposal continues to be in abeyance, victim to a mix of community opposition, political squabbling and the ambition of a now privatised Sydney Airport to retain its monopoly of interstate and international flights.

Another noisy intrusion, commercial tourist helicopters, has gained a presence in the World Heritage Area. These joy flights reverberate in the mountain valleys despite the voluntary Fly Neighbourly Agreement requesting aircraft to fly at more than 300 metres above the ground. The gorges of the Blue Mountains are a greater depth than the flying height permitted by the Agreement, enabling helicopters to fly well below the cliff tops, much to the annoyance of other tourists and local residents. The Environment Protection Authority has secured noise controls preventing joy flights over the Three Sisters, but flights are still permitted in the Grose and Kanangra-Boyd Wilderness areas and to resorts in the Megalong Valley. In the last ten years, fortunately, joy flights have not increased, mainly because of local community opposition and limited interest by tourists in expensive helicopter rides.

Even more destructive of the amenity of the Blue Mountains was the promotion of joy flights using superseded military jet aircraft operating at near supersonic speeds to within 150 metres of the ground. These flights involved mock attacks on 'targets' in the mountains, so that unsuspecting park visitors were 'dive bombed' while they camped on lonely mountain tops. Bob Debus, NSW Minister for the Environment, was incensed at these flights and wrote to Senator Hill, Federal Minister for the Environment, saying that 'to contemplate the environment being disrupted and invaded in this manner beggars belief'. The Australian Fighter Flight Centre had its permit to operate removed in November 2002. Alas, the Flight Centre and a new operator have re-established these raids on the Blue Mountains.

Mining and Logging Abuse

Public disapproval of mining in national parks is so great that the Greiner Government, in order to claim green credentials, banned it through legislation introduced by Tim Moore in 1989. Mining, however, continues to damage areas proposed for national park protection in the Greater Blue Mountains area.

The Newnes Plateau, north of Lithgow, is subject to several coal mining enterprises, and has caused the land surface above the mines to subside by two metres as almost the entire coal seam is removed in the mining process. Mine subsidence has destroyed groundwater aquifers, drained streams, and damaged hundreds of clifflines, pagodas and upland swamps on the Plateau. The Wollangambe River, a tributary of the Colo River, is being badly polluted by the discharge of more than 14 megalitres a day of groundwater from the Clarence Colliery near Bell although Centennial Coal, the owner of the Colliery, has admitted that the pollution is unacceptable. Its October 2000 environmental impact

The Grose River is enclosed by a sandstone escarpment.

statement for a greatly expanded colliery proposed no solution to the problem. Planning NSW was alerted to the problem by conservationists and it has requested that mine expansion be deferred until the pollution is mitigated.

The Plateau also faces exploitation from two mines that supply sand to the Sydney and Blue Mountains construction industry. The mining has caused downstream sediment pollution of the Wollangambe River. Newnes Plateau contains a number of botanically interesting shrub swamps that are also threatened with sand mining, including a recent proposal at Newnes Junction nearby. The sand resources around Mellong Swamps on Tinda Creek, north of Windsor and east of the Wollemi Wilderness, are also being exploited, risking increased sediment pollution of the Colo River.

Logging for firewood, fence posts and timber has put the Newnes Plateau and Mount Coricudgy under environmental stress. The largely undisturbed eastern side of Mount Coricudgy is within the Wollemi Wilderness. At 1,256 metres, the summit of Mount Coricudgy is the highest point in the northern Blue Mountains and has great botanical value due to its stands of majestic Southern Blue Gum and rainforest, and it is the source of seven wild streams.

Pipelines, Pests, Inholdings, Highways, Dams and Off-road Vehicles

The proposal for a gas pipeline through the Wollangambe Wilderness was defeated in the 1960s when the Colong Foundation demonstrated that an alternative route via the Southern Highlands would be feasible, but electricity, gas and telecommunication easements through the wilderness have remained on the agenda ever since. In the most recent example, in April 2001, Ian Armstrong, the Member for the State seat of Lachlan, proposed not only another gas pipeline easement, but also a six-lane highway. The highway was originally proposed to go through the Blue Labyrinth section of Blue Mountains National Park. Later proposals were for a route through parkland on the Darling Causeway, a Bells Line of Road upgrade, and a tunnel beneath the mountain towns that would have cost several billion dollars. Premier Bob Carr rubbished Armstrong's original proposal, but later a $2 million full feasibility study, jointly funded by the State and Federal Governments, was supported to consider options for a superhighway to the west. The superhighway proposal appears unlikely to succeed, as projected traffic levels do not justify the duplication of the existing highway; however, a modified scheme, diverting the existing highway north over Newnes Plateau and bypassing Lithgow, is more likely to emerge as a threat to the World Heritage property.

The desire to 'drought-proof' Sydney has inspired many inappropriate proposals for dams in the Blue Mountains. In 1984, the Department of Water Resources examined dam sites within the Wollemi Wilderness which included a Wheeny Creek dam and two on the Colo River, to augment water supplies for Sydney and the Gosford-Wyong region. A $300 million proposal to raise the Warragamba Dam wall, which would have meant the flooding of the Lower Kowmung and Coxs Rivers, was rejected by the Carr Government in 1995 in favour of a $90 million auxiliary spillway for the dam. The need for more wilderness flooding dams within the World Heritage Area has so far been avoided through the development of improved water use and more effective user-pays schemes for Sydney residents.

The use of four wheel drives (4WDs) in the World Heritage Area cannot but be highly detrimental to the natural environment if fire trails in national parks are opened to these high-impact vehicles. They introduce weeds, cause large scale soil erosion (e.g. 'the Face,' a steep hill on the Wirraba Trail near Wollemi Creek) and damage fragile ecosystems such as swamps. The roads used by 4WDs act as barriers to some wildlife, facilitate theft of bush rock that provides essential reptile habitat, enable access for rubbish and car dumping, and allow feral animals to penetrate the area more quickly. Once established, these rough tracks take years to revegetate. Off-road vehicles are easily able to carry generators, chainsaws, firearms and dogs, all of which are inconsistent with appreciation of the natural environment. Even blatantly illegal acts by some 4WD drivers are virtually impossible to monitor and manage due to the size and isolation of the Heritage Area. A 1979 State Pollution Control Commission inquiry into the recreational use of off-road vehicles found that 'the use of vehicles in areas of virgin country can cause immeasurable damage to flora and fauna, cutting deep impressions as vehicles tyre-spin their way to gain traction over rough terrain. Narrow trails are widened, hillsides are rut-scarred, front-end winches ropescar and ruin vegetation, archaeological relics are damaged and the possibility of fires is increased from vehicles and the activities of users of vehicles'.

Despite the overwhelming evidence of damage caused by these vehicles, the National Parks and Wildlife Service completed a Memorandum of Understanding with 4WD clubs in October 2000 which enables their members to drive on previously restricted roads, such as the one that passes through the Couridjah Corridor in the Nattai area, closed to public vehicle access for a generation.

Horseriding is another threat to the fragile sandstone environment of the Blue Mountains. Studies of the recreation impacts caused by walkers and horses demonstrate that horses are responsible for much of the damage to the bush. Each horse is 8–10 times heavier than a person. The horse's sharp, steel-shod hooves break up tracks, exposing them to rapid erosion. They cause stream sedimentation and introduce weeds and manure into pristine areas, particularly river flats. The parking areas for horse floats, trucks and associated horse yards are also part of the impacts of horseriding in national parks. These impacts are relatively isolated at the moment, but the promotion of the National (horseriding) Trail, which runs along the western side of the Blue Mountains, would encourage horseriding and become a cause for concern. The Trail passes through the Gardens of Stone National Park, where environmental impacts arising from horseriding are more likely due to its difficult terrain and fragile rock formations, particularly if commercial horseriding tours become established.

The presence of private freehold land within the World Heritage Area continues to provide opportunities for inappropriate 4WD access to wilderness areas and unauthorised grazing where stock wander into the adjoining national park from unfenced private lands, particularly within the Wollemi and Yengo National Parks. Inappropriate tourism development could be established on such inholdings and cause a significant loss of wilderness values in areas such as at Konangaroo Clearing on the Coxs River, where there are huts associated with horseriding and with fishing parties that are flown in by helicopter.

Riparian weeds, including willows, and pest animals such as pigs, deer, horses, goats and cattle, are an increasing problem in the World Heritage Area, a problem that is exacerbated when private enclaves in the park are stocked with these animals. Willows and other weeds can choke up previously open streams and provide feed to pest animals which then increase soil disturbance and pollution problems. Pest control programs have successfully removed most of the willows from the Colo and Kowmung Rivers, but other pests, such as foxes and cats, are proving more difficult to manage.

Yet another major threat to World Heritage values is the practice of burning off private bushland adjoining national parks to encourage grass cover in order to provide rough grazing for stock. Several major and highly destructive fires in the north of the Greater Blue Mountains World Heritage Area can be attributed to this cause. Heavy penalties have been introduced to discourage the lighting of such fires.

World Heritage listing will probably facilitate tourist development and thus increase the risk of private lands being used for exclusive resorts within wilderness areas. Provisions guaranteeing access to private lands within national parks have unfortunately increased the risk of inappropriate development in these areas. However, provided resort and residential developments are not approved in sensitive areas, tourism need not be an insurmountable environmental problem. Voluntary acquisition of remaining private properties within the World Heritage Area should in time reduce risk of inappropriate development and damage. National park management plans, required under NSW legislation, can also prevent damage caused to parkland by overuse.

CHAPTER 9

Celebration and Dedication

ON 12 May 2001 a celebration and dedication ceremony attended by some 2,500 people was held at Govetts Leap, Blackheath. Seating, catering, transport and other facilities were efficiently organised by the NSW National Parks and Wildlife Service. The gathering was addressed by five of the key figures in the accomplishment of the Blue Mountains World Heritage listing: the Hon. Bob Debus, NSW Minister for the Environment and State Member for the Blue Mountains, Dr Geoff Mosley, author of the original proposal, Senator Robert Hill, Federal Minister for the Environment, Councillor Jim Angel, Mayor of Blue Mountains City Council, representing the 14 local government areas affected by listing, and Mr Peter King, Chairman of the World Heritage Committee.

In a broad-ranging speech, Bob Debus encapsulated the environmental commitment of the community that ultimately brought about World Heritage Listing:

'The campaign to see this region declared a World Heritage Area began more than a decade ago and this ceremony is the culmination of a great deal of hard work by many dedicated individuals, conservationists, government officials, parliamentarians and community groups. It is a tremendous privilege to stand here tonight as NSW Environment Minister and local member to share with the world what those who live here have always known – that the Blue Mountains is one of the most special places on earth.

'We stand today somewhere near the heart of a massive 250 million year old conservation zone of wild gorges, sandstone plateaus, basalt outcrops, relic plants, forests and swamps – more than a million hectares stretching from the Hunter to the Southern Highlands. An area one third the size of Belgium.

'The World Heritage nomination was successful on the grounds of the richness of this area's biological and ecological quality and because it protects habitat of many endangered species.

'But to all of us the Greater Blue Mountains also has profound values of cultural association.

'There is a distinct tradition of voluntary conservation in this region, which follows an immensely longer tradition of the Aboriginal community.

'The cultural, spiritual and environmental significance of the Mountains has been recognised by the Gandangara and Dharuk people – by the Darkinjung, Wonnarua, Awabakwal, Dharawal and Wiradjuri – for at least 14,000 years. Their occupation is seen in more than 700 recorded Aboriginal sites, and today we work to establish closer partnership with indigenous communities as the custodians of this great land.

'The Valley below us was reserved in 1875. But that still did not mean it was safe. Just over 70 years ago a group of bushwalkers, including Alan Rigby, Dorothy Lawry and the great Myles Dunphy, mounted a campaign to save the Valley's Blue Gum Forest from clearing.

'The Sydney Bush Walkers' fight was probably the first 'Save the Forest' campaign of its type in Australia – and the genesis of the long, determined struggle that has resulted among other things in the World Heritage listing. Andy MacQueen records in his history of the Grose Valley that soon after the reservation of the Blue Gum Forest the Federation of Bushwalking Clubs in NSW was formed because bushwalkers realised that more united effort would be needed to save other areas.

'The passion ignited by a handful of conservationists here in the Blue Mountains in 1930-32 has grown and galvanised over the ensuing years. Today we have this vast network of eight public reserves – the Blue Mountains, Kanangra-Boyd, Wollemi, Gardens of Stone, Yengo, Thirlmere Lakes and Nattai National Parks and the Jenolan Caves Karst Conservation Reserve.

A classic Blue Mountains view: the cliff lines of Mt Solitary and Narrow Neck Peninsula above a mist-covered Jamison Valley.

'The Blue Mountains has indeed always held a distinct place in the European Australian ethos.

'Read the accounts of the early explorers – not just Blaxland, Lawson and Wentworth – but earlier adventurers like George Bass, George Caley and Francis Barralier – of Strezlecki and Mitchell. Read Hugh Speirs' book *Landscape Art and the Blue Mountains* (foreword by C. Manning Clark and preface by John Olsen) which traces the evolution of Australian landscape art through two centuries of Australian painting in the Mountains – from Conrad Martens to Fred Williams.

'See the authors who have lived here or written about the Mountains – Charles Darwin, taking a break from the voyage of the *Beagle*; Henry Lawson; Eleanor Dark; Sumner Locke Eliot; Kylie Tennant; Patrick White's *Night on Bald Mountain*; and Delia Falconer's recent novel. Too many even to try to list. You see today nature and art run together in the Blue Mountains.

'It's part of my job to thank the individuals, agencies and community groups that have brought us here today:

'Tim Hager and all the staff of the National Parks and Wildlife Service of NSW who have for 40 years cherished and protected these lands and passionately supported the nomination process at every level of their expertise.

'The staff of Environment Australia, who performed so brilliantly in the final negotiations with the World Heritage Committee.

'Our local organisations, the members of the Blue Mountains World Heritage Committee, not least Jane Aiken.

'The members of the Blue Mountains Conservation Society, not least Les Coyne.

'Successive mayors, councillors and staff of the City of Blue Mountains – who were at key times supported by surrounding councils including Penrith, Hawkesbury, Wollondilly, Wingecarribee, Lithgow, Oberon, Mudgee, Cessnock and Singleton.

Narrow Neck, Mount Solitary, and Kings Tableland on the horizon.

A tranquil pool on the Grose River.

'There has been 10 years of bipartisan political support – Pam Allan, Maggie Deahm, and John Faulkner, Kerry Bartlett, Tim Moore and Robert Hill.

'With all the detachment I can muster I would say to you that two Premiers have had critical roles in the establishment of these lands for conservation – Neville Wran and Bob Carr.

'Dozens of scientific experts have contributed absolutely critically. They include Barbara Briggs, Teresa Jones and the staff of the Botanical Gardens, Jamie Kirkpatrick, Brian Marshall and the pre-eminent botanists from around the world who actively supported the nomination in the critical stages.

'There are individual conservationists who in various ways played special roles – Geoff Mosley who prepared the scientific and political case for nomination; Joan Domicelj who prepared the nomination report; Jim Somerville and the late Bing Lucas who inspired her.

'The people who have come by their life work to define conservation in the Mountains – Milo Dunphy and Wyn Jones.

'The Colong Foundation – Tom Widdup, the iconic Dot Butler and the man who first had vision for World Heritage here, Alex Colley. When the nomination was approved Bob Carr sent Alex a hand written note: "Very few people", he said, "are able to deliver something as grand as the vast protected areas of the Blue Mountains to future generations".

'Finally, there is Colong's Director – Keith Muir – the dedicated unstoppable campaigner who never gave up and, as I have said before, has been the glue that held a ten-year effort across half of Australia together. He deserves an acknowledgment now.

'The Greater Blue Mountains is a living record of major stages in the earth's history. It is often described as a natural laboratory for the study of evolution, particularly of Australia's great eucalypts. The Greater Blue Mountains contains 91 eucalypt species, or 13 per cent of those in the world. Twelve species are believed to exist only in the Sydney sandstone region and one of these has just two known individuals, making it perhaps the rarest species in the world. It is fitting then that the successful nomination of the Greater Blue Mountains recognises the outstanding universal significance of our eucalypt forests.

'Biological time capsules hidden in this ancient land still protect remnant Gondwana species. National Parks ranger David Noble's discovery in 1994 of the Wollemi Pine, a species thought to be extinct for two million years, and Wyn Jones' recognition of this living fossil, are world renowned. More recently, two more stands have been found sheltering in Wollemi National Park. And we can only speculate what else this 500,000 hectare wilderness laboratory is still protecting.

'World Heritage Listing will, without a doubt, increase international appreciation of the Blue Mountains area and through that foster support for its protection and encourage more visitors to the area. It binds Governments to the preservation of the World Heritage qualities of the region.

'So, although this World Heritage Dedication Ceremony is an historic celebration and a major achievement for conservation, it also marks a new beginning.

'The Greater Blue Mountains region lies on the edge of Sydney and is under constant threat from the pressures associated with urbanisation and population growth. Strong legislation and effective partnerships between the community and all levels of Government are needed to keep these pressures at bay.

'The Great Grose Gorse Walk, Streamwatch, Willows out of Wollemi, the Rural Fire Service, WIRES, the Blue Mountains Wild Plant Rescue Service, the Regent Honeyeater Recovery Group and the revitalisation of Katoomba and Echo Point are examples of strong community and government programs. Without these programs and the support of dedicated volunteers, the job of Government would be far more difficult.

'This week we have taken another substantial step forward.

'I have approved the adoption of plans of management for Blue Mountains, Nattai, Kanangra-Boyd and Wollemi National Parks. The Yengo National Park and Parr State Recreation Area draft plan

Hanging Rock, upper Grose Valley.

of management are on public exhibition and I have approved the adoption of the Special Areas Strategic Plan of Management under the *Sydney Water Catchment Management Act*.

'What this means is that today – the day the World Heritage is declared – the National Parks and Wildlife Service has before it an action plan for conserving almost 900,000 hectares of this area and four of the eight reserves contained within it.

'These plans of management for the national parks recognise the importance of the region to cyclists, walkers, tourism operators, horse riders and local communities, particularly in the Blue Mountains National Park, which attracts three million visitors a year. More than 40,000 people a year visit the spectacular Kanangra-Boyd National Park, many of them overnight campers.

'However, the plans are ultimately conservation documents and identify the specific pressures facing every part of every park. They prioritise programs to alleviate these pressures. In Kanangra-Boyd the plan proposes to declare the Kowmung, Jenolan and Kanangra River systems wild and scenic and control caving in bat nursery caves. In all parks, high priority will be given to the eradication of specific pests, the protection of water catchment, the preservation of threatened species and the protection of wilderness contained in each reserve. Nattai National Park alone contains 30,000 hectares of wilderness, the first such area declared under the *Wilderness Act, 1987*. In all parks where activities such as horseriding and cycling are allowed, minimal impact codes of conduct will be developed.

'These plans will form the basis of a wider strategic plan by State and Commonwealth governments and eventually a plan of management for the entire World Heritage Area. It is our international obligation to do this. With the work done already we can meet these obligations much faster than ever done before.

'Tonight, I am particularly pleased to confirm that the Government will shortly proclaim the 38,000 hectare Grose Wilderness in the valley below us; it is only proper that the nomination has been made by the Confederation of Bushwalking Clubs NSW.

'I can find no better words to express what this declaration means than to turn again to Andy MacQueen, who says this: "If the Grose Wilderness Area comes into being… generations to come will be able to explore its hidden recesses, or sit and contemplate it in solitude, without further threat from new roads or tourist developments… and wonder that the place has survived intact. And they will continue to gaze from the lookouts into the Cradle of Conservation."

'The Grose Wilderness has survived intact. The world has formally recognised the heritage and beauty of our Blue Mountains and we are its proud guardians.

'Future generations from around Australia and the world can continue to come to the lookouts and gaze. There is no greater environmental legacy we can bequeath them. Thank you.'

At the same event, Dr Geoff Mosley said:

'The Blue Mountains is a land of superlatives, something people who know the area have realised for a long time. Now the world is finding out. Here is my list for these mountains: 1) The world's best display of how sandstone mountains evolve; 2) Outstanding scenery including the world's largest wilderness of its type; 3) One of the world's most significant and diverse eucalypt-dominated forests; 4) Incredibly important cultural values, the wider sandstone region contains thousands of Aboriginal carvings on flat rock platforms – the greatest concentration in Australia and probably in the world; and 5) Above all, in terms of what we are celebrating this evening, it is one of the world's best examples of a more recent caring relationship, between the community and the natural world, developed over many generations. If you like, it is a world-class centre of excellence for this.

'Needless to say, all these attributes, not just the vegetation, deserve international recognition and after allowing a bit of time for the assessors to complete their education (and helping them to do it) I believe this area should be renominated in respect of additional criteria and extended boundaries for its

Warm temperate rainforest lines a gully in the central Blue Mountains.

significance for the understanding of the evolution of land forms, for the beauty of its natural scenery, and for its cultural landscape values.

'I am truly honoured to be invited to speak at this gathering as a person representative of community groups. I cannot imagine a greater honour.

'Those who were involved with the campaign for World Heritage recognition were as varied as the area's flora. They included community and government bodies at all geographic levels – local, state and national (including politicians, public servants and scientists). All pulled their weight and worked in a cooperative way.

'What has been achieved is typical of many of the earlier conservation efforts here, extending over 15 decades. World Heritage was a logical culmination of all the earlier work, which involved such things as building the most complex track system in the world, creating the first big national parks and wilderness areas, researching the environment, and defending the country against inappropriate developments, including quarries, mines, dams, a gas pipe line (through the Wollangambe Wilderness) and pine plantations on the Boyd Plateau.

'As with all these early stages, the move for World Heritage involved leadership. On this occasion the Colong Foundation showed the way. Its World Heritage campaign was launched by Bob Carr in 1989. It saw things through to the end and is continuing the work.

Mount Solitary, Blue Mountains National Park.

Point Cameron, above the Capertee Valley, Gardens of Stone National Park.

'Most appropriately local people in this part of the world took up the cause with enthusiasm. We often fail to recognise the important, often crucial, role played by councils, but in this case there can be no excuse for ignorance.

'A local World Heritage Committee was formed, the Blue Mountains Conservation Society put its shoulder to the wheel, the Blue Mountains City Council developed a very pro-active campaign of its own which included community education and lobbying of the Federal Government. As with many of the previous endeavours in the Mountains the breadth and depths of the efforts were exceptional.

'The task and the challenges continue. It is very much an evolving situation. If the progressive new national heritage system proposed by the Federal Minister, Robert Hill, is established, as I hope it is, the Blue Mountains will need to be renominated on the new national list for all its superlative values.

'World and national heritage listing can provide a new focus for management. While many unsuitable proposals have been rejected, others got through and the consequent land uses will need to be dealt with in a way which gives priority to all these values. It provides also a chance to consolidate.

'One of the most encouraging things to me in contemporary society is the widespread public support for national parks and wilderness areas – 99% at the last reckoning. They have the same status with the community as schools and hospitals.

'This gives me hope. These areas not only provide us with the opportunity to maintain our links with the environments of our evolutionary past but through the understanding and respect they engender they can help provide a bridge to a more environmentally friendly relationship in the future.

'In the Blue Mountains this fact is probably more evident than anywhere else. Another good reason for celebrating today! Thank you.'

Senator Hill announced that the Commonwealth Government would provide $1 million towards the construction of a Greater Blue Mountains World Heritage Interpretive Centre, which would act as a gateway to 'the stunning Blue Mountains World Heritage Area, showing the internationally recognised biodiversity of this magnificent natural asset'. The new centre would showcase the Blue Mountains natural assets, the more than 90 eucalyptus species, breathtaking views, deep valleys, and, of course, the famous Wollemi Pine. He said that the Commonwealth would provide half the salary costs of a new position within the NPWS to coordinate matters relative to the Heritage area and that the Commonwealth would progress a renomination with regard to the cultural values.

Mr Peter King, Chairman of the World Heritage Committee, described how impressed the Committee had been with the attributes of the Mountains, and said he rated the Mountains above other projects nominated for listing.

Blue Mountains Mayor, Jim Angel, called the ceremony: 'The Blue Mountains proudest day. This is the most significant historical day in the history of the Blue Mountains. We are the only city on the planet that is surrounded and enclosed by a World Heritage listed national park'. The Blue Mountains Council had resolved that the City will be known as 'The City within a World Heritage National Park'.

❑ ❑ ❑

Sixty-five years after the publication of Myles Dunphy's vision to protect the vast wilderness areas of the Blue Mountains it has been realised as the Greater Blue Mountains World Heritage Area.

Cascades over rock shelves are a common sight along the escarpments of the Central Blue Mountains.

Index

Aboriginal sites, 2, 92, 112, 118
Airly-Genowlan Mesa, 68, 76-83
Aiken, Jane, 114
Allan, the Hon. Pam, 70, 82, 87, 88, 90, 94, 104, 108, 116,
Alliance for Airport Location Outside Sydney, 108
Allison, Senator Lyn, 92
American Journal of Science and Arts, 3
Angel, Mr Jim, 112, 122
Angus Place Colliery, 78-82
Animal Protection Act, 6
Ashworth, Prof., 102
Askin Government, 20, 24-28
Associated Portland Cement Manufacturers (Aust.) (APCM), 18-20, 28-34, 42
Armstrong, Mr Ian, 110
Awabakwal, 112
Australian Alps, 100
Australian Fighter Flight Centre, 108
Australian Forestry Council, 45
Australian Heritage Commission, 90
Australia Party, 26
Autobric Pty Ltd, 56

Baal Bone Colliery, 82
Badgerys Creek Airport proposal, 96, 100, 106-108
Badgery, Ms Rosyln, 70
Balanced development, 28, 34
Barlow, Dr Brian, 92
Barralier, Francis, 114
Bartlett, Kerry, 116
Bass, George, 114
Batsh Camp, 54
Beale, the Hon. Minister for Conservation, 24, 28, 48
Bell, Michael, 60, 84
Bellingham, S R, 4
Bells Line of Road, 52, 110
Benson, Doug H, 4
Bindook Gorge, 12
Bindook Highlands, 12, 27
Birds Protection Act, 6
Birds and Animals Protection Act, 6
Black, Denise, 48
Blackfellows Hand Cave, 78
Blackheath, 106, 112
Blackwell, David, 78
Blue Circle Cement, 28-30
Blue Gum Forest, 7, 12, 14, 18, 102, 112
Blue Labyrinth, 12, 110
Blue Mountains and Burragorang Map, 14
Blue Mountains Ash, 17, 78
Blue Mountains City Council, 80, 87-88, 102, 104, 105, 112, 114, 122
Blue Mountains City Council, World Heritage Listing Sub-Committee, 88
Blue Mountains Conservation Society, 70, 92, 104, 114, 122
Blue Mountains Echo, 8
Blue Mountains for World Heritage Committee, 88, 114, 122
Blue Mountains for World Heritage, 2, 84-90
Blue Mountains National Park, 13, 16, 27, 74, 85, 96, 104, 106, 110, 112, 118, 120

Blue Mountains Wild Plant Rescue Service, 116
Bodington Hill, 104
Bonnum Pic, 10, 74
Boorai Ridge, 56
Bouchenaki, Mr Mounir, 96
Boyd Plateau, 16, 18, 22, 26-28, 36-50, 70, 120
Branagan, Dr, 34
Briggs, Barbara, 116
Bungonia Gorge, 32-34
Bushfires, 104-105
Bushwalker conservation movement, 2
Burragorang Valley, 18, 74, 105
Butler, Dot, 116

Caley, George, 114
Canoe Creek, 64
Canyon Colliery, 104
Capertee River, 52
Capertee Valley, 76, 80, 82, 121
Carr Government, 82, 96, 110
Carr, the Hon. Bob, 2, 66, 74, 78, 80, 84, 88, 92, 110, 116, 120
Carrick, Sir John, 28
Catholic Bushwalkers Club, 22
Catholic priests' petition, 28
Cave-in, 34
Centennial Coal, 82, 108
Cessnock Council, 114
Church Creek, 20, 22-24, 34
Clarence Colliery, 80, 108
Clear Hill, 16
Cleary, W J, 12
Clough, Mr Mick, 82
Cocks, Mr, 40
Coffey, Mr Eric, 48
Colo Committee, 52-66, 78
Colo-Hunter Wilderness, *see* Wollemi Wilderness
Colo River, 52, 53, 56-63, 108, 110
Colo Shire Council, 52
Colo Wilderness, 60
Colong Bulletin, 22, 26, 28-30, 46
Colong Caves, 16, 18-34, 40, 42, 54
Colong Committee, *see* Colong Foundation
Colong Foundation, 2, 22, 26-34, 38-50, 54, 66-82, 84-88, 92-96, 104-110, 116, 120
Colong Maze, 12
Commercial tourist helicopters, 108, 111
Commission of Inquiry into the Airly Colliery proposal, 80
Commission on National Parks and Protected Areas, 84
Confederation of Bushwalking Clubs, *see* Federation of Bushwalking Clubs
Cooke, Mr Arthur, 14
Coricudgy State Forest, 52
Corral Swamp, 16
Cotton, Senator, 44
Couridjah Corridor, 10, 18, 68, 111
Cox, Graham, 84
Coxs River, 110, 111
Coyne, Mr Les, 114
Crabtree, the Hon., 58-60
CSR-Readymix, 70-72

Culoul Range, 54
Cultural associations, 1, 2, 87, 88, 92, 112, 118, 120, 122
Cumberland County Council, 2
Cunninghamia, 4

Daly, Dr T J, 8
Dana, Dwight, 3, 86
Dark, Eleanor, 114
Darkinjung, 112
Darwin, Charles, 3, 86, 114
Deahm, Maggie, 116
Debus, the Hon. Bob, 2, 87, 104, 108, 112
Democratic Labor Party, 45
Department of Conservation, 36
Department of Environment and Planning, *see* Planning NSW
Department of Lands, 14, 36
Department of Mineral Resources, 18, 24, 28, 58, 64, 70, 82
Department of Mines, *see* Department of Mineral Resources
Department of Water Resources, 110
Dharawal, 112
Dharuk, 112
Diamond Falls, 16
Doctors' petition, 28
Domicelj, Joan, 94, 116
Dungalla Cascades, 38
Dunphy, Milo, 20-26, 32, 40, 52, 72-76, 102, 116
Dunphy and Loder Architectural Partnership, 18, 102
Dunphy, Myles, 10-16, 18, 68, 78, 112, 122

Eades, Mr Mike, 104
Earth Sanctuaries, 104
Eden, David, 26, 32
Einfeld, Sid, 26
Electricity Commission (Elcom), 56-64
Elements of the Past, 8
Elenius, Elizabeth, 26, 42
Elenius, Kaj, 46
Environment Australia, 96-98, 114
Environment Protection Authority (EPA), *see also* State Pollution Control Commission; 76, 108
Eucalyptus genera, 1-2, 86-87, 92, 100, 116, 118, 122

Fahey, the Hon. John, 68, 70, 82, 88
Fairmont Resort, 102-104
Falconer, Rodney, 78
Faulkner, the Hon. Senator John, 90, 116
Federation of Bushwalking Clubs, 18-20, 78, 112, 118
Fife Cave, 24
Fife, Mr Wal, 20-28
Figgis, Penny, 82
Fisher, Howard, 80
Fish River, 38
Fly Neighbourly Agreement, 108
Forestry Act, 1916, 38
Forestry Commission, 16, 28, 36-50, 68
Forestry Department, *see* Forestry Commission

Four wheel drive vehicles, 12, 70, 110, 111
Fragar, Mr Max, 88
Freudenstein, Mr, 48
Friends of Nattai, 70
Fuller, the Hon. John, 44

Gallop, Bert, 10
Gandangara, 112
Gangerang, 12, 29
Gardens of Stone, 68, 76-82, 83, 102
Gardens of Stone National Park, 75, 79, 80-82, 111, 114
Georges River by-election, 1970, 26
Glen Davis, 52
Gormley, Jenni, 84
Gospers Mountain, 10, 60
Goulburn River, 52
Govetts Leap, 12, 102, 104, 112
Grand Canyon of NSW, 52
Grassby, the Hon. Al, 45
Greater Blue Mountains National Park proposal, 1934, 10-16, 18, 68, 78
Greater Blue Mountains World Heritage Area, 74, 111, 122
Greater Blue Mountains World Heritage Interpretive Centre, 122
Great Grose Gorse Walk, 116
Greiner, the Hon. Nick, 70-76, 88, 108
Grose Valley, 4, 7, 8, 10, 12, 85, 103, 112, 117
Grose Wilderness, 14, 99, 101, 104, 108, 118

Hager, Mr Tim, 114
Hansell, Mr Allan, 70
Hartcher, the Hon. Chris, 88
Hatton, Mr John, 74
Hawke, the Hon. Bob, 88
Helman Report, 54, 62, 66
Hills, Mr Pat, 26, 58
Hill, the Hon. Senator Robert, 96-98, 108, 112, 116, 122
Hilltop, 68, 106
Horseriding, 12, 90, 111, 118
Howard Government, 92, 94
Howard, the Hon. John, 28
Hungerford, C.A., 12
Hunter Valley, 10, 52, 56, 112

ICOMOS (International Council on Monuments and Sites), 96
Institute of Architects, 20, 34
IUCN (World Conservation Union), 66, 84, 87, 94, 96-100

Jabiluka, 94, 98
Jamieson, L N, 24
Jenolan Caves, 8, 10, 36, 38
Jenolan Caves Karst Conservation Reserve, 112
Johnson, Prof. R N, 20
Jones, Ms Teresa, 116
Jones, Mr Wyn, 116

Kakadu National Park, 94-98
Kanangra-Boyd National Park, 5, 18-34, 36-50, 68, 96, 112, 116

Kanangra-Boyd Wilderness, 12, 16, 18, 21, 36, 50, 54, 87, 108
Kanangra Road, 36, 38
Kanangra Walls, 16, 36, 38
Kane, the Hon. Senator, 45
Katoomba, 16, 36, 70, 105, 116
Katoomba Council, 16
Katoomba Daily, 10
Katoomba Echo, 78
Kedumba Valley, 102
Keen, N F A, 22
Keith, David H, 4
King, Mr Peter, 112, 122
Kings Tableland, 94
Kirkpatrick, Prof. Jamie, 90, 92, 116
Konangaroo Clearing, 111
Konangaroo State Forest, 26, 28, 36-50
Kosciuszko, 10, 36
Kowmung River, 18, 23, 24, 36, 43, 110, 111, 118

Lake Burragorang, 68, 70
Lambs Creek, 78
Land and Environment Court, 72-74
Landa, the Hon. Paul, 60-66
Lapstone Monocline, 84
Laurie Montgomery Consulting Engineers, 24
Laurie, Montgomery and Petit Report, 46
Lawry, Dorothy, 112
Laws, Mr John, 60
Lees, Senator Meg, 92
Leura Golf Course, 102
Lewis, the Hon. Tom, 20, 28
Linden Creek, 104
Lithgow, 76-78, 108, 110
Lithgow Council, 82, 114
Lo Po, Fay, 87
Lord, Stephen, 78
Lower Blue Mountains Conservation Society, 78
Lucas, H C (Bing), 1, 116

McAndrew, Wayne, 82
McArthurs Flat, 70
McCartney, Mr Roy, 28
McClellan QC, Peter, 72
Macdonald, Dr Peter, 74, 82
Macdonald Wilderness, *see* Yengo Wilderness
Mackerras, Mr Neil, 45
Maclean, Madi, 70
Macqueen, Andy, 112, 118
Maldon cement works, 18, 32
Manning, Peter, 46
Marshall, Prof. Brian, 92, 116
Marulan, 30, 34
May, Prof. Sir Robert, 96
Megalong Valley, 108
Mellong Swamps, 110
Meredith, Mrs Charles, 3
Meredith, Peter, 102
Metherell, Dr Terry, 74-76, 88
Metropolitan Cement Company, 18-20, 28
Mining Act, 1992, 80
Minister for Defence, 60
Mirrar Aboriginal people, 94

Mittagong, 10, 36, 68, 70, 106
Moore, Ms Clover, 74, 82
Moore, the Hon. Tim, 70-76, 84, 88, 104, 108, 116
Morris, Mr Barry, 84
Morris, the Hon. Milton, 50
Mosley, Dr Geoff, 1, 2, 84-92, 112, 116, 118
Mount Alexandra, 10
Mount Armour, 20, 22, 26-28, 30, 40, 50
Mount Boonbourwa, 10
Mount Colong, 19, 22, 70
Mount Coricudgy, 110
Mount Cumbertine, 10
Mount Flora, 68-76
Mount Misery, 72
Mount Victoria, 8, 106
Mount Werong, 10
Mountain Trails Club, 10, 12, 18
Mudgee Council, 114
Muir, Keith, 68, 72-76, 82, 94, 96, 108, 116
Mulock, Mr Ron, 62

Narrow Neck Peninsula, 16, 98, 113, 114
National Herbarium, 58, 88, 92
National Parks Association, Berrima Branch, 70
National Parks Association of NSW (NPA), 16, 20-22, 36-38, 54, 60, 66, 68, 78
National Parks and Primitive Areas Council, 10, 18
National Parks and Wildlife (Amendment) Bill, 1969, 26, 38, 42-44
National Parks and Wildlife Amendment Act, 2001, 82
National Parks and Wildlife Service (NPWS), 16, 24, 28, 56, 58, 66, 78, 88, 96, 111, 112, 114, 118, 122
National Trail, 111
National Trust, 20, 48, 68, 78
Native Animals Protection Act, 6
Nattai Foundation, 70
Nattai National Park, 68-74, 112, 116, 118
Nattai River, 68-72, 106
Nattai Valley, 12, 18, 68-70
Nattai Wilderness, 70-76, 106, 118
Natural Sketches of New South Wales, 3
Nature Conservation Council of NSW, 20, 88
Newcom Collieries, 78
Newnes Plateau, 58-64, 76-80, 106, 108, 110
Newnes State Forest, 82
Nexus Environmental Studies Pty Ltd, 102
Noble, David, 66, 116
North Thurat, 12
Northern Blue Mountains, 52, 60, 64, 86, 88, 110
Novacoal, 80-82
NSW Government Railways, 8

Oberon Council, 114
Ollier, Prof. Cliff, 90-92

Pagodas, 78-82, 108
Parkes, Sir Henry, 8
Parr State Recreation Area, 116

Permo-Triassic period, 84-86
Pest control, 111
Petersen, Mr George, 42-44
Petition to Parliament, 20
Phillips, Prof. Adrian, 100
Picton, 68
Pine Planting Program in NSW, 44-45
Pinnacles State Park Proposal, 78
Pinus insignis, 38
Pinus radiata, 38
Pipers Flat, 60
Planning NSW, 102, 110
Platypus, 4, 6, 100
Primitive Areas, *see also* wilderness; 10-12
Prineas, Peter, 60
Putty Road, 52
Putty State Forest, 62

Radiata Plateau, 104
Railway Guide, 1879, 8
Recher, Dr Harry, 56
Regent Honeyeater Recovery Group, 116
Rentoul, Laurence, 32
Reserve 29837, 18
Reserve 67062, 16, 36, 44
Reserve 68800, 18
Residential Bushland Conservation zone, 104
Residential Bushland zone, 104
Rigby, Alan, 12, 112
Rigby, Roger, 84
Robertson, Margaret, 70
Rocky Creek Canyon, 82
Routley, R and V, 45
Royal Botanic Gardens, 88, 92, 116
Rudder, Roy, 10
Ruddock, Mr Max, 26
Rural Fire Service, 116

Schliecher, Ruth, 8
Sclerophyll Open Forest, 1, 86-87
Second South Pacific Parks Conference, 60
Sewerage tunnel, 96, 105-106
Sinclair, John, 96
Singleton Council, 114
Smith, Dick, 54, 60
Smith, J and P, 8
Softwoods Forestry Agreements Bill, 1972, 45
Soil Conservation Service, 24
Somerville, Jim, 30, 116
Southern Highlands, 70, 108, 110, 112
Special Areas Strategic Plan, 118
Springwood, 87
Starlight's Track, 70
State Cabinet, 20, 26, 64, 74

State Council of the Liberal Party, 26-28, 42
State Pollution Control Commission (SPCC), 48-50, 54-58, 111
Stein, Justice Paul, 72
Stern, Mr Terry, 32
Sullivan, Ms Sharon, 90
Swartz, the Hon., 45
Sydney Basin, 84, 86
Sydney Bush Walkers, 12, 18, 112
Sydney Speleological Society, 22
Sydney Water Board, 70-72
Sydney Water Catchment, 2, 68-70, 104, 118
Sydney University Conservation Society, 20, 28
Sydney University Liberal Club, 26

Ten Years with Palette, Shotgun and Rifle, 4
The 10.7% Report, 50
The Edge, 94
The Three Sisters, 6, 108
The Wilderness Sydney Forgot, 60
Theiss Bros, 18
Thirlmere Lakes, 68
Thirlmere Lakes National Park, 112
Thompson, Pat, 84
Thorsell, Dr Jim, 87, 94-100
Threlfo, George, 70
Tierney, Father James, 22
Tierney, Senator, 92
Timber Industries Ltd, 45
Tinda Creek, 110
Tomat Heights, 12
Tonkin, Mr, 26
Total Environment Centre (TEC), 52, 54, 60, 66, 68
Tourism, 2, 8, 10, 16, 52, 111
Tourist open areas, 12
Townshend, George, 52
Trickett, Mr O, 24

UNESCO (United Nations Education, Scientific and Cultural Organisation), 1, 66, 84, 87, 94, 96
United Mine Workers Union, 82
Upper Colo, 52
Uren, the Hon. Tom, 45

Walker, Brian, 26, 42
Walking tracks, 8, 70
Wanganderry Tableland, 70, 74, 106
Warragamba Club, 10
Warragamba Dam, 70, 96, 105, 110
Warragamba Water Supply Catchment, 68
Warringah Council, 34
Wattle Ridge, 68
Weatherley, Mark, 26, 42

Webster, the Hon. Robert, 68-70, 80
Weiley, John, 94
Wheeny Creek, 110
Whitehouse, John, 60, 72, 78
Whitlam, the Hon. Gough, 45
Widden Brook, 52
Widdup, Tom, 94, 96, 116
Wild Dog Mountains, 12, 37
Wilderness, 1, 2, 10, 12, 20, 36, 52, 56, 60-66, 87-88, 96, 102-111, 116-122
Wilderness Act, 1987, 66, 68, 76, 118
Wilderness and Power, 60
Wilderness in Australia, 54
Wilderness in Danger, 60
Wilderness Society, The, 66
Wilderness Working Group, 64
Williwa Creek, 60
Wingecarribee Shire Council, 70-72, 114
Winmalee, 105
Wiradjuri, 112
Wirraba Trail, 60, 110
Wolgan Gap, 78
Wollemi Creek, 52, 56, 110
Wollemi National Park, 60-66, 68, 78, 82, 111, 112, 116
Wollemi Pine, 1, 66, 67, 87, 88, 100, 116, 122
Wollemi Wilderness, 2, 52-67, 80, 87, 108, 110
Wollemi Wilderness Plan, 66
Wollondilly Council, 114
Wombat Pinch, 10
Wonnarua, 112
Woodford, James, 66
World Heritage Bureau, 94, 96
World Heritage Centre, 84, 94
World Heritage Committee, 1, 94-100, 112, 114, 122
World Heritage Conference, 94
World Heritage Convention, 94-98
World Heritage Dedication Ceremony, 102, 112, 116
World Heritage Management Symposium, 96
World Heritage Properties Ministerial Committee, 90
World Plan Executive Council, 104
Wran, the Hon. Neville, 54-56, 64, 78, 104, 116
Wrigley, John, 70

Yengo National Park, 111, 112, 116
Yengo Wilderness, 52
Yerranderie Peak, 10

Zeigler, Oswald, 104